MongoDB 4 Quick Star

Learn the skills you need to work with the world's most popular NoSQL database

Doug Bierer

BIRMINGHAM - MUMBAI

MongoDB 4 Quick Start Guide

Commissioning Editor: Amey Varangaonkar
Acquisition Editor: Reshma Raman
Content Development Editor: Kirk Dsouza
Technical Editor: Shweta Jadhav
Copy Editor: Safis Editing
Project Coordinator: Hardik Bhinde
Proofreader: Safis Editing
Indexer: Tejal Daruwale Soni
Graphics: Jason Monteiro
Production Coordinator: Jyoti Chauhan

First published: September 2018

Production reference: 1260918

Published by Packt Publishing Ltd.
Livery Place
35 Livery Street
Birmingham
B3 2PB, UK.

ISBN 978-1-78934-353-3

www.packtpub.com

To Siriporn Jamikorn, my friend, lover, roommate, interpreter, business partner, constant companion, life partner, and wife of 21 years, who passed away while I was writing this book.

– Doug Bierer

`mapt.io`

Mapt is an online digital library that gives you full access to over 5,000 books and videos, as well as industry leading tools to help you plan your personal development and advance your career. For more information, please visit our website.

Why subscribe?

- Spend less time learning and more time coding with practical eBooks and Videos from over 4,000 industry professionals

- Improve your learning with Skill Plans built especially for you

- Get a free eBook or video every month

- Mapt is fully searchable

- Copy and paste, print, and bookmark content

Packt.com

Did you know that Packt offers eBook versions of every book published, with PDF and ePub files available? You can upgrade to the eBook version at `www.packt.com` and as a print book customer, you are entitled to a discount on the eBook copy. Get in touch with us at `customercare@packtpub.com` for more details.

At `www.packt.com`, you can also read a collection of free technical articles, sign up for a range of free newsletters, and receive exclusive discounts and offers on Packt books and eBooks.

Contributors

About the author

Doug Bierer is the owner and CTO of *unlikelysource*, a website development and consulting company that over the last 10 years has developed 60+ websites for customers around the world. In addition, Doug has been a contract trainer for RogueWave Software/Zend Technologies since 2009. He wrote his first program in 1971 on a PDP-8, and has developed commercial applications in languages including Assembler, C, C++, Java, JavaScript, Perl, and PHP. He developed a video series on MongoDB for InfiniteSkills (now part of O'Reilly Media) in 2014. Before diving into MongoDB, Doug developed applications and performed administration for MySQL databases. He has continued to develop applications that access MongDB to this day.

I would like to thank Siriporn Jamikorn, my beloved wife of 21 years, for being there for me in spirit, and who would have been proud of this work. I would also like to thank Nannapas Jamikorn for providing inspiration and hope.

About the reviewer

Andrew Caya started programming computers in GW-BASIC and QBASIC in the early 1990s. Before becoming a PHP developer almost 10 years ago, he did some software development in C, C++, and Perl. He is now a Zend Certified PHP Engineer and a Zend Certified Architect. He is also the creator of *Linux for PHP*, the lead developer of a popular Joomla extension, and a contributor to many open source projects.

He is currently CEO, CTO, and founder of *Foreach Code Factory*, an instructor at *Concordia University*, the author of *Mastering the Faster Web with PHP, MySQL, and JavaScript*, and a loving husband and father.

Packt is searching for authors like you

If you're interested in becoming an author for Packt, please visit `authors.packtpub.com` and apply today. We have worked with thousands of developers and tech professionals, just like you, to help them share their insight with the global tech community. You can make a general application, apply for a specific hot topic that we are recruiting an author for, or submit your own idea.

Table of Contents

Preface

MongoDB can solve problems considered difficult if not impossible for aging **Relational Database Management System (RDBMS)** technologies. In order to properly use this technology, a major thought-paradigm shift needs to take place. This guide will address this issue by showing readers how to quickly and easily obtain results for even the most complex modeling tasks. Most computer professionals have been trained to use RDBMS, but are unsure of how to properly use MongoDB. One important thing that this book explores is how to properly model and use data in a *NoSQL* environment. Examples focus on PHP and JavaScript as both are widely used on internet web servers, and are well understood by the majority of IT professionals.

Who this book is for

This book is intended for DevOps professionals, web developers, IT professionals, **Database Administrators (DBAs)**, job seekers looking to transition their careers into the database with a future, and technical managers who want to get a clue as to what their techs are talking about.

What this book covers

Chapter 1, *Introducing MongoDB*, discusses *NoSQL*, provides an overview of MongoDB, and ends by covering detailed installation procedures for Windows as well as various forms of Linux servers. Also covered in this chapter, in addition to a discussion of the benefits of using MongoDB, are *big picture* questions including *what* is it and *why* use it.

Chapter 2, *Understanding MongoDB Data Structures*, covers foundational aspects of MongoDB database design, including documents, fields, and collections. Comparisons are drawn between SQL and MongoDB terminology. At the end of this chapter, you will learn how to create a MongoDB database.

Chapter 3, *Using the Mongo Shell*, of especial interest to DBAs, covers how to use the *mongo* shell to connect to a MongoDB database and perform CRUD (Create, Read, Update and Delete) operations. Plenty of JavaScript examples are provided.

Chapter 4, *Developing with Program Language Drivers*, goes through how to access a MongoDB database using PHP. Up until this point, examples are using JavaScript. In this chapter, the focus shifts to programming language driver access. This chapter will be of great interest to developers. Even if your main language is not PHP, the examples can be easily understood.

Chapter 5, *Building Complex Queries Using Aggregation*, addresses complex queries. The focus of this chapter will be on a feature unique to MongoDB called *aggregation*. This facility allows database developers or DBAs to return subsets of data grouped, sorted and filtered, running through a multi-stage pipeline. Plenty of JavaScript examples are provided.

Chapter 6, *Maintaining MongoDB Performance*, focuses on performance features such as indexing and sharded clusters. In addition, there is a substantial discussion on backup, restore, and replication. Solid working examples are shown, providing detailed steps that show you how to create a replica set as well as a sharded cluster.

Chapter 7, *Securing MongoDB*, shows how to secure the database itself, add users, and adjust permissions to specific collections. You will also learn how to enforce authentication and create an admin user. In addition, we address how to configure MongoDB to use SSL/TLS using x.509 certificates.

Chapter 8, *Getting from Web Form to MongoDB*, presents an *end-to-end* example using the PHP language driver. You will see how data posted from a web form is added to the database over a secure communications link, with security enabled. After that, you will see how a simple query is implemented showing the new entry. In addition, this chapter shows how to launch AJAX requests and have MongoDB respond using PHP.

To get the most out of this book

It is expected that the reader has access to a computer running any of the major operating systems, including Windows, macOS, and Linux. MongoDB does not need to be installed before you start reading: the first chapter will give you detailed installation instructions.

A basic knowledge of *JavaScript* is assumed. You should have some idea of JavaScript syntax, but do not have to be a guru.

PHP knowledge is not required, but will be useful to understand the examples in chapters 4 and 8. PHP syntax is very close to that of the *C language*, and was chosen because most developers are familiar with either PHP or C.

A knowledge of the *SQL* language is not required, but may be helpful to understand some of the analogies given in the book to help aid understanding of key MongoDB concepts.

Likewise, a knowledge of *RDBMS* systems is not required, but might help the reader at a foundational level.

Installation instructions and information you need for getting set up are provided in the first chapter.

Download the example code files

You can download the example code files for this book from your account at www.packt.com. If you purchased this book elsewhere, you can visit www.packt.com/support and register to have the files emailed directly to you.

You can download the code files by following these steps:

1. Log in or register at www.packt.com.
2. Select the **SUPPORT** tab.
3. Click on **Code Downloads & Errata**.
4. Enter the name of the book in the **Search** box and follow the onscreen instructions.

Once the file is downloaded, please make sure that you unzip or extract the folder using the latest version of:

- WinRAR/7-Zip for Windows
- Zipeg/iZip/UnRarX for Mac
- 7-Zip/PeaZip for Linux

The code bundle for the book is also hosted on GitHub at https://github.com/PacktPublishing/MongoDB-4-Quick-Start-Guide. In case there's an update to the code, it will be updated on the existing GitHub repository.

We also have other code bundles from our rich catalog of books and videos available at https://github.com/PacktPublishing/. Check them out!

Download the color images

We also provide a PDF file that has color images of the screenshots/diagrams used in this book. You can download it here: https://www.packtpub.com/sites/default/files/downloads/9781789343533_ColorImages.pdf.

Conventions used

There are a number of text conventions used throughout this book.

`CodeInText`: Indicates code words in text, database table names, folder names, filenames, file extensions, pathnames, dummy URLs, user input, and Twitter handles. Here is an example: "Mount the downloaded `WebStorm-10*.dmg` disk image file as another disk in your system."

A block of code is set as follows:

```
use <dbName>;
  db.<collection>.insertOne({ // document });
  or
  db.createCollection(<collection>);
```

Any command-line input or output is written as follows:

```
sudo pecl install mongodb
```

Bold: Indicates a new term, an important word, or words that you see onscreen. For example, words in menus or dialog boxes appear in the text like this. Here is an example: "Select **System info** from the **Administration** panel."

 Warnings or important notes appear like this.

 Tips and tricks appear like this.

Get in touch

Feedback from our readers is always welcome.

General feedback: If you have questions about any aspect of this book, mention the book title in the subject of your message and email us at customercare@packtpub.com.

Errata: Although we have taken every care to ensure the accuracy of our content, mistakes do happen. If you have found a mistake in this book, we would be grateful if you would report this to us. Please visit www.packt.com/submit-errata, selecting your book, clicking on the Errata Submission Form link, and entering the details.

Piracy: If you come across any illegal copies of our works in any form on the Internet, we would be grateful if you would provide us with the location address or website name. Please contact us at copyright@packt.com with a link to the material.

If you are interested in becoming an author: If there is a topic that you have expertise in and you are interested in either writing or contributing to a book, please visit authors.packtpub.com.

Reviews

Please leave a review. Once you have read and used this book, why not leave a review on the site that you purchased it from? Potential readers can then see and use your unbiased opinion to make purchase decisions, we at Packt can understand what you think about our products, and our authors can see your feedback on their book. Thank you!

For more information about Packt, please visit packt.com.

Introducing MongoDB

This chapter gives you a brief overview of MongoDB, including answering such questions as *what is MongoDB?*, *why use it?*, and *what are its benefits?* It then covers installing the MongoDB Community Edition (free version) on a Windows server and on Linux. You will learn the installation differences between RPM based Linux distributions (Red Hat, Fedora, CentOS) and Deb based (Debian, Ubuntu). There is also a brief summary of how to install directly from source.

The topics that we will learn in this chapter are:

- Overview of MongoDB
- Installing MongoDB
- Installing MongoDB on Linux

Overview of MongoDB

MongoDB represents a radical and much needed departure from *relational* database technology. Dr. Edgar F. Codd (`https://en.wikipedia.org/wiki/Edgar_F._Codd`), an English computer scientist working for IBM, published his seminal paper, A Relational Model of Data for Large Shared Data Banks in 1970. It formed the basis for what we now know as **RDBMS** (**Relational Database Management Systems**), using **SQL** (**Structured Query Language**), adopted by IBM, Relational Software (later Oracle), and Ingres (`https://en.wikipedia.org/wiki/Ingres_(database)`), a research project at the University of California in Berkeley. Ingres, in turn, spawned Postgres, Sybase, Microsoft SQL Server, and others.

The first version of MongoDB was introduced in 2009 by 10gen (`https://en.wikipedia.org/wiki/MongoDB_Inc.#History`) (later MongoDB Inc.) to address a crying need not addressed by the current stable of RDBMS systems, which were, for the most part, based on almost 50-year-old technology; handling big data and modeling objects. Initially proprietary, MongoDB was later released as open source.

DB-Engines (`https://db-engines.com/en/ranking`) provides up-to-date rankings of competing database systems. It is of interest to note that MongoDB is now in the Top 10, currently ranked fifth. However, you should also note that the *score* assigned to MongoDB is 343.79 compared with the number one ranked system, Oracle, with a score of 1,311.25.

Handling big data

One massive problem faced by legacy RDBMS systems is difficulty managing Big Data (`https://en.wikipedia.org/wiki/Big_data`). Examples would include data produced by the NASA Center for Climate Change, the Human Genome Project, which analyzes strands of DNA, or the Sloan Digital Sky Survey, which collects astronomical data. RDBMS systems are designed to maximize storage, which was an expensive resource 50 years ago. In the 21st century, storage costs have dropped dramatically, making this a secondary consideration. Another aspect of RDBMS systems is their ability to provide flexibility by way of creating *relations* between tables, which by its very nature introduces overheads, compounded when handling big data.

MongoDB addresses the needs of big data by incorporating modern algorithms such as map reduce (`https://en.wikipedia.org/wiki/MapReduce`), which allows for parallel distributed processing on a cluster of servers. In addition, MongoDB has a feature referred to as sharding, which allows fragments of a database to be stored and processed on multiple servers.

It should be noted that although MongoDB is designed to handle big data, it is actually more of a general purpose platform. If your *only* need is to handle big data, it might be worth your while to investigate Apache Cassandra (`https://cassandra.apache.org/`) with Hadoop (`http://hadoop.apache.org/`), which is expressly designed to handle massive amounts of data.

Modeling objects without SQL

A classic paradox in **object oriented programming (OOP)** code that requires database access is caused by the two-dimensional architecture of the traditional RDBMS. The two dimensions, *rows* and *columns*, are in turn grouped into *tables*, much like a legacy spreadsheet. In order to achieve the *third* dimension one needs to perform resource intensive joins and form relationships between tables. In order to map programming object classes to the database, incredible programmatic gymnastics are required to achieve the goal.

With MongoDB, there is no rigid database schema you must adhere to. Instead of rows you insert *documents*. A set of documents is referred to as a *collection*. Each document can directly model an object class, which in turn greatly facilitates the work of storing and retrieving from the database.

MongoDB has its own rich query language, which can perform tasks similar to what the developer might expect from a legacy RDBMS using SQL. Because MongoDB does not use SQL, it is often referred to as a *NoSQL* database.

 For an excellent introduction to *NoSQL*, its underlying philosophy and its ramifications, a highly recommended resource can be found in the NoSQL Guide (`https://martinfowler.com/nosql.html`) on Martin Fowler's website.

Installing MongoDB

For the purposes of this book, we focus on the *MongoDB Community Edition* for the simple reason that it's free of charge. This version is also an excellent way to get your feet wet, so to speak, allowing you to learn about and experiment with MongoDB risk free. Before beginning installation, be sure to check the minimum requirements for your operating system in the MongoDB installation manual: `https://docs.mongodb.com/manual/installation/`.

 On a live server, in a commercial enterprise, it is recommended you use the *MongoDB Enterprise Advanced* version. You might also consider two cloud-based offerings, *MongoDB Atlas* or *MongoDB Stitch*. The former provides a cloud-hosted MongoDB database service. The latter builds upon the former, opening the MongoDB API so that your apps can make calls and receive responses.

Installing MongoDB on Windows

The version featured in this book is MongoDB 4.0. The minimum requirement for a Windows installation is *Windows Server 2008 R2*, *Windows 7*, or later.

 The MongoDB reference manual warns that *Windows Server 2008 R2* or *Windows 7* require a hotfix patch be installed to prevent errors from occurring under certain conditions. For more information see: `https://support.microsoft.com/en-gb/help/2731284/33-dos-error-code-when-memory-memory-mapped-files-are-cleaned-by-using`.

Download and install

To download and install MongoDB on Windows, proceed as follows:

1. Go to the MongoDB download center at: `https://www.mongodb.com/download-center#community`.
2. Select the appropriate operating system where it says *Version.*
3. Click on **DOWNLOAD (msi)**:

4. When prompted, choose **Save File**.
5. Click on the saved MSI file to start the installer.
6. Click **OK** when the security prompt appears asking to **Open Executable File?**
7. Click **Run** when the security warning appears.
8. Click **Next** to start the MongoDB Setup Wizard.
9. Read the license agreement and click on the checkbox and **Next**. Note that if you do not accept the license agreement the installation will terminate.
10. When asked **Choose Setup Type**, for the purposes of this illustration, select **Complete**. *MongoDB Compass*, which is a handy utility which greatly facilitates database management, is automatically installed.
11. Now that all choices have been made, click on **Install** and click **Yes** when the **User Account Control** security warning pops up.

12. As of MongoDB v4.0, the installation wizard lets you configure startup options. If you want to have MongoDB start automatically and run in the background, choose **Run service as Network Service user**. You can also configure the directory where MongoDB stores its data files (**Data Directory**), and where log files are stored (**Log Directory**):

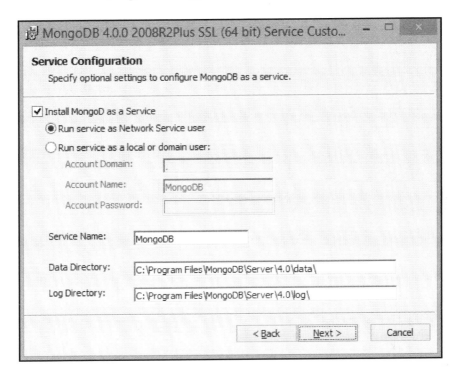

13. Click **Next** to continue and **Finish** when the installation completes.

MongoDB Compass

Assuming you elected to install the complete package, *MongoDB Compass* will auto-launch once the installation completes. You will need to scroll down through its license agreement (separate from the license agreement for MongoDB itself), and click **Agree**. You can follow and then close the initial help tutorial, and also set **Privacy Settings** that control whether or not you will be sending crash reports, usage statistics, and requesting automatic updates to/from MongoDB Inc.

This utility is described in more detail in the Chapter 2, *Understanding MongoDB Data Structures*, We also use this utility to create our first database and collection (see following sections). Here is the *Compass* screen as seen on Windows:

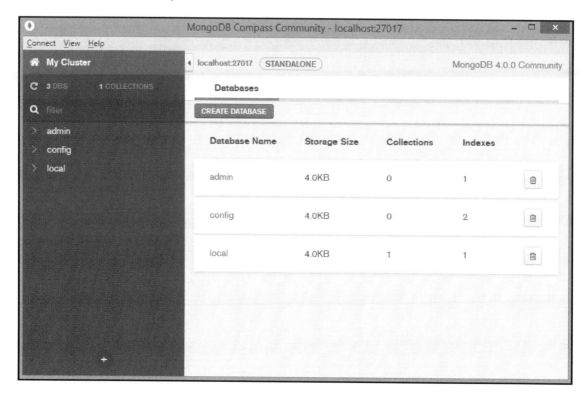

MongoDB Windows file locations

If using the Windows MSI installer (recommended), the MongoDB program files will be stored here:

```
C:\Program Files\MongoDB\Server\<version>
```

You have the option, during the installation process, of specifying the location where the database and log files are stored. Once finished, here is a look at the new directory structure:

```
                            MINGW64:/c/Users/george            -  □  ×

george@asus-windoze MINGW64 ~
$ ls -1 /c/Program\ Files/MongoDB/Server/4.0/
total 132
drwxr-xr-x 1 george 197121     0 Jul  5 15:56 bin/
drwxr-xr-x 1 george 197121     0 Jul  5 16:01 data/
-rw-r--r-- 1 george 197121 34520 Jun 21 20:53 GNU-AGPL-3.0
-rw-r--r-- 1 george 197121  2149 Jun 21 20:53 LICENSE-Community.txt
drwxr-xr-x 1 george 197121     0 Jul  5 15:59 log/
-rw-r--r-- 1 george 197121 16726 Jun 21 20:53 MPL-2
-rw-r--r-- 1 george 197121  2195 Jun 21 20:53 README
-rw-r--r-- 1 george 197121 57190 Jun 21 20:53 THIRD-PARTY-NOTICES

george@asus-windoze MINGW64 ~
$
```

 If you elected to install MongoDB as a service, it starts automatically, and can be administered just as any Windows service.

The configuration file, which contains the locations of the database and log files, defaults to:

```
C:\Program Files\MongoDB\Server\4.0\bin\mongod.cfg
```

This file is automatically generated by the installer. By default, here are its contents:

```
                mongod.cfg - C:\Program Files\MongoDB\Server\4.0\bin - Geany          -  □  ×

 File  Edit  Search  View  Document  Project  Build  Tools  Help

 mongod.cfg ✖
  1  # mongod.conf
  2
  3  # for documentation of all options, see:
  4  #    http://docs.mongodb.org/manual/reference/configuration-options/
  5
  6  # Where and how to store data.
  7  storage:
  8    dbPath: C:\Program Files\MongoDB\Server\4.0\data
  9    journal:
 10      enabled: true
 11  #  engine:
 12  #  mmapv1:
 13  #  wiredTiger:
 14
 15  # where to write logging data.
 16  systemLog:
 17    destination: file
 18    logAppend: true
 19    path:  C:\Program Files\MongoDB\Server\4.0\log\mongod.log
 20
 21  # network interfaces
 22  net:
 23    port: 27017
 24    bindIp: 127.0.0.1
```

Installing MongoDB on Linux

It is important to understand the MongoDB installation process on Linux, even if you are a developer or IT professional and are not using Linux personally, it's extremely likely that the internet-facing server you or your customer use is running Linux. W3Techs (`https://w3techs.com/`), a company that does web technology surveys, estimates that in 2018, the running on Linux was at 68.1% compared with 32% for Windows.

There are three primary considerations when installing MongoDB on Linux, each of which we will address in turn:

- Linux based upon Debian and Ubuntu
- Linux based upon RedHat, Fedora, and CentOS
- Installing directly from source code

 With the bewildering array of Linux distributions currently available, it is difficult to decide which version to feature for the purposes of demonstrating MongoDB on Linux. A significant number of Linux distributions are based on either *Debian* or *Red Hat* Linux. Accordingly, this section covers installing MongoDB on both. A website which gives good insight on all reported Linux distributions is DistroWatch (`https://distrowatch.com/`). Linux Mint (`https://linuxmint.com/`), although now extremely popular, wasn't included here, as it's Debian-based and not as commercially available as Ubuntu.

Installing on Debian or Ubuntu Linux

Debian Linux (`https://www.debian.org/`), self-described as the universal operating system, is a free open-source project that uses a fork of the Linux kernel, and draws heavily upon GNU (`http://www.gnu.org/software/software.html`, for example, GNU Not Unix) software. Ubuntu Linux (`https://www.ubuntu.com/`) is produced by the Canonical Group Ltd based in South Africa, and is based upon Debian. For the purposes of this book, we will focus on *Ubuntu* version 18.04, code-named Bionic Beaver, released in April 2018, a designated **LTS (Long Term Support)** version.

The preferred way to install any given software on Ubuntu is to use a Debian package. Such packages have the extension `*.deb` and include a script that tells the package management program where to place the pre-compiled binary files as they are extracted. Popular package management programs include synaptic (`http://www.nongnu.org/synaptic/`, graphical interface, resolves dependencies, and does a lot of "housekeeping"), aptitude (`https://help.ubuntu.com/lts/serverguide/aptitude.html`, like *synaptic* but has a textual, command-line menu), and `apt-*` (that is `apt-get` (`https://linux.die.net/man/8/apt-get`), `apt-key` so on: very fast, command-line only). For the purposes of this section we will use `apt-get`.

 Ubuntu provides its own MongoDB package, which is what gets installed if you simply run `sudo apt-get install mongodb`. To get the latest "official" version directly from MongoDB, you should follow the procedure outlined as follows. If you already have installed the Ubuntu `mongodb` package, you will need to first uninstall it before proceeding.

The MongoDB packages available for Ubuntu/Debian include the following:

`mongodb-org-server`	Primary MongoDB system daemon
`mongodb-org-mongos`	MongoDB *shard* routing service
`mongodb-org-shell`	MongoDB shell
`mongodb-org-tools`	Provides various `mongo*` tools for import, export, restore, and so on.

In addition, a composite package, `mongodb-org`, which contains all four of these packages, is provided.

Package installation

To install MongoDB on an Ubuntu/Debian server, you will need *root* access. A unique feature of Debian-based Linux distributions is that direct login as root is not allowed for security reasons. Accordingly, you can promote yourself to root using `su`, or you can precede the various commands with `sudo`, which instructs the OS to process this command as root.

Please proceed as follows:

1. Import the public key from the MongoDB key server. This is needed so that the package manager can authenticate the MongoDB package:

```
ed@ed: ~
File  Edit  View  Search  Terminal  Help
ed@ed:~$ sudo apt-key adv \
>      --keyserver hkp://keyserver.ubuntu.com:80 \
>      --recv 9DA31620334BD75D9DCB49F368818C72E52529D4
[sudo] password for ed:
Executing: /tmp/apt-key-gpghome.cyD3ZMdcdj/gpg.1.sh --keyserver hkp://keyserver.ubuntu.com:80
 --recv 9DA31620334BD75D9DCB49F368818C72E52529D4
gpg: key 68818C72E52529D4: public key "MongoDB 4.0 Release Signing Key <packaging@mongodb.com
>" imported
gpg: Total number processed: 1
gpg:               imported: 1
ed@ed:~$
```

2. Add the MongoDB repository to the Linux server's sources list:

```
ed@ed: ~
File  Edit  View  Search  Terminal  Help
ed@ed:~$ echo \
> "deb [ arch=amd64,arm64 ] https://repo.mongodb.org/apt/ubuntu xenial/mongodb-org/4.0 multiverse" \
> | sudo tee /etc/apt/sources.list.d/mongodb-org-4.0.list
deb [ arch=amd64,arm64 ] https://repo.mongodb.org/apt/ubuntu xenial/mongodb-org/4.0 multiverse
ed@ed:~$
```

 The commands listed should be on one line. We use a backslash (\) to indicate a line of text that is too long to fit the printed page. When typing the command, omit the backslash (\) and do not hit enter until the command has been fully entered.

3. Refresh the package database from the sources list by running:

`sudo apt-get update`

 Ubuntu version 18.04 is code-named *bionic*. You will note this name is used in step #2 here, where the MongoDB repository is added to the *sources* list. If this source is not found, you will receive an error message: **The repository ... bionic/mongodb-org/4.0 ... does not have a Release file** In this situation, substitute the code name xenial (Ubuntu 16.04) in place of bionic (Ubuntu 18.04).

4. Install the latest (stable) version of MongoDB. Here, we install only the composite package, which alleviates the need to separately install the four primary packages listed previously:

```
sudo apt-get install -y mongodb-org
```

 You will note, at the end of the installation, that the installer creates a user `mongodb` who belongs to a group `mongodb`, which is also newly created. This is the system user MongoDB uses when it runs.

Configure and run MongoDB on Ubuntu/Debian

If you followed the procedure outlined in the previous section, a configuration file `/etc/mongod.conf` will have been auto-generated by the installation script. By default, data files will be placed in `/var/lib/mongodb` and log files in `/var/log/mongodb/mongod.log`:

```
mongod.conf [Read-Only]
                        /etc
Open ▾   ⊞                                    Save   ≡  ● ● ●

# mongod.conf

# for documentation of all options, see:
#   http://docs.mongodb.org/manual/reference/configuration-options/

# Where and how to store data.
storage:
  dbPath: /var/lib/mongodb
  journal:
    enabled: true
#  engine:
#  mmapv1:
#  wiredTiger:

# where to write logging data.
systemLog:
  destination: file
  logAppend: true
  path: /var/log/mongodb/mongod.log

# network interfaces
net:
  port: 27017
  bindIp: 127.0.0.1

        Plain Text ▾   Tab Width: 8 ▾      Ln 18, Col 18   ▾   INS
```

You are now able to perform these operations:

Operation	Command
Start | stop | restart the server	sudo service mongod start|stop|restart
Get the server status	sudo service mongod status
Access MongoDB via the shell (covered later)	mongo --host 127.0.0.1:27017

Here you can see the server started, along with its status:

```
                                   ed@ed: ~
File Edit View Search Terminal Help
ed@ed:~$ sudo service mongod start
ed@ed:~$ sudo service mongod status
● mongod.service - MongoDB Database Server
   Loaded: loaded (/lib/systemd/system/mongod.service; disabled; vendor preset: enabled)
   Active: active (running) since Thu 2018-07-05 13:50:31 BST; 4s ago
     Docs: https://docs.mongodb.org/manual
 Main PID: 19500 (mongod)
   CGroup: /system.slice/mongod.service
           └─19500 /usr/bin/mongod --config /etc/mongod.conf

Jul 05 13:50:31 ed systemd[1]: Started MongoDB Database Server.
Jul 05 13:50:33 ed mongod[19500]: 2018-07-05T13:50:33.829+0100 I CONTROL  [main] Automatically disabling TL
S 1.0, to force-enable T
```

 MongoDB installation scripts now automatically bind MongoDB to localhost (IP address 127.0.0.1) for security reasons.

Installing on Red Hat, Fedora, or CentOS Linux

Red Hat, Fedora, and CentOS have a relationship similar to that of Debian and Ubuntu. Red Hat (https://www.redhat.com/en) is the original company behind this distribution, producing its first release in 1995. In addition to making improvements in the graphical interface and overall management of Linux, Red Hat is known for its RPM (Red Hat Package Management) technology. In this corner of the Linux world, packages are bundled into files with the extension *.rpm, and contain installation instructions, which makes the installation, updating, and management of Linux software much easier.

Fedora (https://getfedora.org/) is a free open source version of what is now **RHEL (Red Hat Enterprise Linux)**. Fedora and the Fedora Project are sponsored by Red Hat, and serve as a test bed for innovation, which, when stable, is ported to RHEL. Fedora Linux releases tend to have rapid development cycles and short lifespans. CentOS (https://www.centos.org/) is also affiliated with Red Hat, and is allowed direct use of RHEL source code. The main difference is that CentOS is free, but support is only available via the community (which is to say, you are on your own!). For the purposes of this book we will use CentOS version 7.

Package installation

The MongoDB packages available for RHEL/Fedora/CentOS are exactly the same as those described in preceding sections for Debian/Ubuntu. Also, as described earlier, a composite package called mongodb-org that contains all four packages is available. Because RHEL/Fedora/CentOS packages use RPM for packaging, the tool of choice for installation, updating and management of packages is **yum (Yellowdog Updater, Modified)**.

To install MongoDB on RHEL/Fedora/CentOS Linux distributions, proceed as follows:

1. Create a repository file for *yum* in the /etc/yum.repos.d directory. The filename should be like this, mongodb-org-X.Y.repo, where X is the major version number for MongoDB, and Y is the minor release. As an example, for MongoDB version 4.0, the current version as of this writing, the filename would be:

    /etc/yum.repos.d/mongodb-org-4.0.repo:

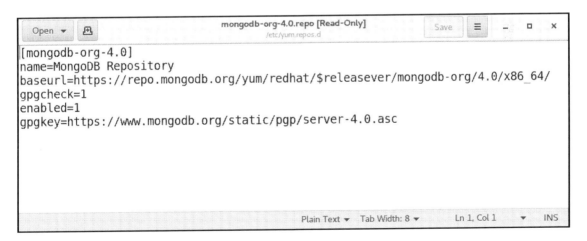

```
[mongodb-org-4.0]
name=MongoDB Repository
baseurl=https://repo.mongodb.org/yum/redhat/$releasever/mongodb-org/4.0/x86_64/
gpgcheck=1
enabled=1
gpgkey=https://www.mongodb.org/static/pgp/server-4.0.asc
```

2. Install the composite package using: `sudo yum install -y mongodb-org`:

```
                              ned@ned:/home/ned                        _  □  ✕
 File  Edit  View  Search  Terminal  Help
[root@ned ned]# sudo yum install -y mongodb-org
Loaded plugins: fastestmirror, langpacks
Loading mirror speeds from cached hostfile
 * base: centos.ustc.edu.cn
 * extras: mirror.kku.ac.th
 * updates: mirror.kku.ac.th
base                                                 | 3.6 kB     00:00
extras                                               | 3.4 kB     00:00
mongodb-org-4.0                                      | 2.4 kB     00:00
updates                                              | 3.4 kB     00:00
(1/3): extras/7/x86_64/primary_db                    | 150 kB     00:00
(2/3): updates/7/x86_64/primary_db                   | 3.6 MB     00:00
(3/3): mongodb-org-4.0/7/primary_db                  | 8.7 kB     00:00
Resolving Dependencies
--> Running transaction check
---> Package mongodb-org.x86_64 0:4.0.0-1.el7 will be installed
--> Processing Dependency: mongodb-org-tools = 4.0.0 for package: mongodb-org-4.
0.0-1.el7.x86_64
```

Configure and run MongoDB on RHEL/Fedora/CentOS

If you followed the procedure outlined previously, a configuration file `/etc/mongod.conf` will have been auto-generated by the installation script. By default, database files will be placed in `/var/lib/mongodb` and log files in `/var/log/mongodb/mongod.log`. Here is an example of the auto-generated file for MongoDB v4.0 on CentOS 7:

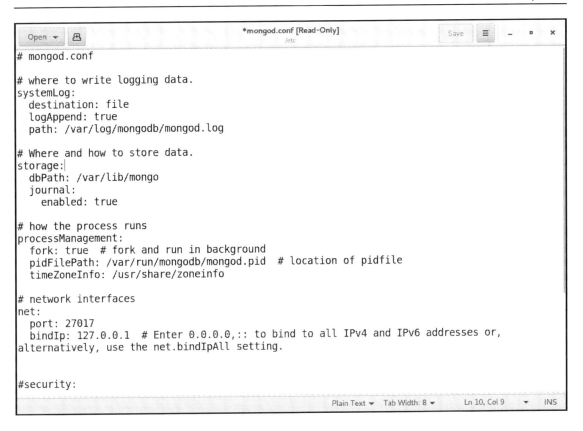

You are now able to perform these operations:

Operation	Command
Start | stop | restart the server	`/bin/systemctl start|stop|restart mongod.service`
Access MongoDB via the shell (covered later)	`mongo --host 127.0.0.1:27017`

After starting the service, use the command `/bin/systemctl status mongod.service` to confirm the status of MongoDB:

```
                              ned@ned:/home/ned                          _  □  ✕

File  Edit  View  Search  Terminal  Help
[root@ned ned]# /bin/systemctl start mongod.service
[root@ned ned]# /bin/systemctl status mongod.service
● mongod.service - MongoDB Database Server
   Loaded: loaded (/usr/lib/systemd/system/mongod.service; enabled; vendor preset: disabled
)
   Active: active (running) since Thu 2018-07-05 14:19:22 BST; 6s ago
     Docs: https://docs.mongodb.org/manual
  Process: 4475 ExecStart=/usr/bin/mongod $OPTIONS (code=exited, status=0/SUCCESS)
  Process: 4472 ExecStartPre=/usr/bin/chmod 0755 /var/run/mongodb (code=exited, status=0/SU
CCESS)
  Process: 4470 ExecStartPre=/usr/bin/chown mongod:mongod /var/run/mongodb (code=exited, st
atus=0/SUCCESS)
  Process: 4468 ExecStartPre=/usr/bin/mkdir -p /var/run/mongodb (code=exited, status=0/SUCC
ESS)
 Main PID: 4479 (mongod)
    Tasks: 26
   CGroup: /system.slice/mongod.service
           └─4479 /usr/bin/mongod -f /etc/mongod.conf

Jul 05 14:19:20 ned systemd[1]: Starting MongoDB Database Server...
```

Installing from source

The beauty of installing MongoDB directly from its source code is that it ensures that you can run MongoDB on *any* server, and that you have the absolute latest version. Minimum requirements for source installation include:

- A *modern* C++ 11 compiler
- Python (https://www.python.org/) 2.7 or above
- pip (https://pypi.org/project/pip/, tool for installing python packages)
- git (https://git-scm.com/, recommended)

In addition, there are OS-specific requirements, which are detailed in this table:

Linux	Compiler: GCC 4.8.2 or later

Red Hat, and suchlike.	Libraries needed:
	`glibc-devel`
	`libcurl-devel`
	`openssl-devel`
	`epel-release`
	`python-devel`

Ubuntu, and suchlike.	Libraries needed:
	`build-essential`
	`libffi-dev`
	`libssl-dev`
	`python-dev`

macOSX	Compiler: Clang 3.4 of XCode 5
	Libraries: XCode (especially command line tools)
Windows	Compiler: Visual Studio 2013 Update 4 or later

It is highly recommended that you carefully read through the source installation process documentation, which can be found on `github.com` at this URL: `https://github.com/mongodb/mongo/wiki/Build-Mongodb-From-Source`.

The source build process does not follow the traditional sequence of **configure**, **make**, and **make install**. Installation is performed using **SCons** (**Software Construction Tool**, `https://www.scons.org/`), which, in turn, uses the programming language Python. Accordingly, after you clone or download the MongoDB source, you will notice many Python scripts and configuration files.

For the purposes of this illustration, we use CentOS 7. To install MongoDB from source, assuming all prerequisites listed previously are met, proceed as follows:

1. Download the source code from `github.com`. There are two ways to download the MongoDB source code from `github.com`:
   1. Download directly from this URL:
      `https://github.com/mongodb/mongo/archive/master.zip`.
      You would then need to unzip it into a folder such as `/home/user/mongo`.

2. If you have installed *git,* you can clone the repository from a command line terminal as follows:

```
[root@ned ned]# git clone https://github.com/mongodb/mongo.git
Cloning into 'mongo'...
remote: Counting objects: 622827, done.
remote: Compressing objects: 100% (466/466), done.
remote: Total 622827 (delta 254), reused 245 (delta 134), pack-reused 622225
Receiving objects: 100% (622827/622827), 398.97 MiB | 10.54 MiB/s, done.
Resolving deltas: 100% (460128/460128), done.
Checking out files: 100% (19634/19634), done.
```

2. Change to the newly created (or cloned) `mongo` directory.

3. Install `pip` requirements:

```
[root@ned mongo]# python -mpip install --user -r buildscripts/requirements.txt
Ignoring mypy: markers u'python_version > "3"' don't match your environment
Ignoring pypiwin32: markers u'sys_platform == "win32" and python_version < "3"' don't match your environment
Ignoring pypiwin32: markers u'sys_platform == "win32" and python_version > "3"' don't match your environment
Collecting cryptography==1.7.2 (from -r buildscripts/requirements.txt (line 2))
  Downloading https://files.pythonhosted.org/packages/99/df/71c7260003f5c469cec3db4c547115df39e9ce6c719a99e0
0e78fd8a/cryptography-1.7.2.tar.gz (420kB)
    100% |████████████████████████| 430kB 1.7MB/s
Collecting jira==1.0.10 (from -r buildscripts/requirements.txt (line 3))
  Downloading https://files.pythonhosted.org/packages/5e/6e/96a299deee19be84d1f6317f71dd86e736b4b3e660e7633c
```

On Windows you would need to run this command:
`pip.exe install -r buildscripts\requirements.txt`

4. Build the source code using SCons:

```
[root@ned mongo]# buildscripts/scons.py all
scons: Reading SConscript files ...
scons version: 2.5.0
python version: 2 7 5 'final' 0
Checking whether the C compiler works... yes
Checking whether the C++ compiler works... yes
Checking that the C++ compiler can link a C++ program... yes
Checking if C++ compiler "g++" is GCC... yes
Checking if C compiler "gcc" is GCC... yes
Detected a x86_64 processor
Checking if target OS linux is supported by the toolchain... yes
```

At this point, you can then follow the same steps listed previously to run MongoDB:

- Create a directory for the database (for example `/var/lib/mongo`)
- Create a directory for the log (for example `/var/log/mongo`)
- Create a config file, which indicates the locations of the database and log (for example `/etc/mongod.conf`)
- Start MongoDB

Summary

In this chapter you gained a better understanding of what MongoDB is, why we use it, and what its benefits are. You then learned how to install MongoDB on both Windows and Linux. You learned how to install the pre-compiled binary packages, which use the extension `*.deb` and are designed for Debian and Ubuntu Linux package manager. In a similar manner, you learned how to install binary packages with the `*.rpm` extension on Redhat, Fedora, or CentOS Linux distributions. Finally, you learned how to install Linux by directly compiling and installing the source code using *SCons* technology.

In the next chapter you will learn about MongoDB data structures, data modeling, and how to create a database, collection, and documents.

Understanding MongoDB Data Structures

2

In this chapter, we will begin with a discussion of NoSQL, which is a cornerstone of the MongoDB philosophy. After that, we will cover the core MongoDB data structures: fields, documents, and collections. We relate these structures to the RDBMS concepts of tables, rows, and columns, but clearly spell out the dangers of trying to apply an SQL solution to a MongoDB database. In addition, we discuss core data-modeling considerations when crafting the structure of your documents and collections. Finally, the chapter ends by showing you how to create a database and collection.

The topics that we will cover in this chapter are:

- What is NoSQL?
- Documents, collections, and databases
- Data-modeling considerations
- Creating a MongoDB database and collection

What is NoSQL?

Before you can begin to use MongoDB properly, it's important to understand its architectural underpinnings. Key to this understanding is what is often referred to as *NoSQL*. As the rubric implies, a NoSQL database does not use SQL language. More importantly, this means that a NoSQL database is free from the legacy, two-dimensional restrictions that handcuff the traditional RDBMS.

There is no formal definition of NoSQL, but there are certain common characteristics. First of all, a NoSQL database does not adhere to the *relational* model. This is evident in that MongoDB has *no fixed schema*, no tables, columns, or rows. A second consideration is that NoSQL databases are driven by the needs of *big data*. Accordingly, NoSQL databases tend to be scalable as well as distributed. This aspect is visible in the MongoDB feature called *sharding*, where *shards* of the database are distributed to a cluster of servers.

Finally, lacking tables, rows, and columns, NoSQL databases use other modeling paradigms. These include:

- **Graph** (https://en.wikipedia.org/wiki/Graph_database): A database technology designed in an almost visual manner, where basic entities that need to be stored are represented as *nodes*. These are connected by *edges*, which can be thought of as lines connecting the various nodes. Finally, there are *properties*, which are like metadata on the nodes. An example of this type is Neo4j (https://neo4j.com/).

- **Key/Value** (https://en.wikipedia.org/wiki/Key-value_database): Where data is stored as *keys* and *values*. This is analogous to a multidimensional array where values can be quickly and easily obtained by simply referencing the key. Some *graph-style* databases make use of this technology internally. An example of this type is Redis (https://redis.io/).

- **Wide column** (https://en.wikipedia.org/wiki/Column_(data_store)): This technology is also analogous to an array with key/value pairs. The difference is that a third element is added; a timestamp. Also, different columns, or even partial columns, can be stored on different servers, lending it to cloud-based computing. An example of this type is Cassandra (http://cassandra.apache.org/).

- **Document** (https://en.wikipedia.org/wiki/Document-oriented_database): The *document-style* database uses what amounts to an object as its smallest logical unit. Multiple documents are stored in a *collection*. Each document can have the same fields, which facilitates querying. On the other hand, as there is no fixed schema, each document could have a different number and type of fields, which contributes to flexibility. An example of this type is MongoDB.

For the most part, NoSQL databases have adopted a two-pronged approach towards development; a *community* edition, and an *enterprise* version. The *community* edition is generally free and open source. As bugs are fixed and features added by the community using it, stable releases are then made available in a paid *enterprise* version. Companies make their money by selling the enterprise version and offering support contracts.

Documents, collections, and database

In order fully to understand how to use MongoDB, it is important to discuss the terms used to describe MongoDB data structures: *documents*, *fields*, and *collections*. The following table summarizes these three terms by way of illustration. In this table, we also draw an equivalence between MongoDB and **RDBMS (Relational Database Management Systems)**:

MongoDB	RDBMS	Illustration
Document	Row	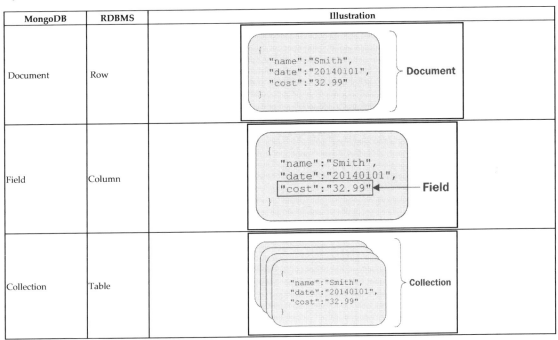
Field	Column	
Collection	Table	

In the preceding example, we see a document that represents information about a member whose name is **Smith**. Within the document are *fields*, the example highlighted being **cost**. Documents that are stored together for a single logical purpose represent a *collection*. A MongoDB *database* consists of one or more collections.

The astute reader will no doubt notice the lack of the MongoDB equivalent to a traditional RDBMS *primary* key. In the RDBMS, it is mandatory for the database developer to define one or more columns as the primary key in order to identify a given row uniquely. This is not required in MongoDB, as a unique identifying field _id is automatically added when the document is inserted into a collection. This field comprises an ObjectId (https://docs.mongodb.com/manual/reference/glossary/#term-objectid) instance and uses a combination of factors to guarantee uniqueness.

Data-modeling considerations

So far, if you are used to traditional SQL-based database systems, you will no doubt be pleased to learn there are direct equivalences between basic data structures, such as fields, documents, and so forth. When it comes to data modeling, on the other hand, a radical departure in thought is needed. We will begin this discussion by comparing a MongoDB *reference* with an *embedded* document.

References

Using *references* (https://docs.mongodb.com/manual/reference/database-references/), it is possible to create a series of related collections in order to establish a *normalized* (https://docs.mongodb.com/manual/core/data-model-design/#normalized-data-models) data model. In the following diagram, a normalized data model is established by defining a field purchId, which forms a reference between the **Customer** collection and **Purchases**. Further, the field itemId can serve as a reference between **Purchases** and **Products**:

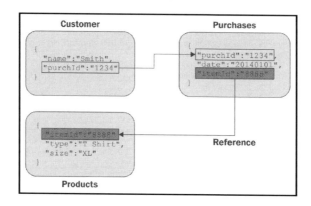

By imposing an SQL-esque solution on a MongoDB dataset, however, you defeat the purpose of using a NoSQL database. Unless your database driver provides support for **DBRefs** (`https://docs.mongodb.com/manual/reference/database-references/#dbrefs`), which allows for an embedded link between collections, you are forced to write code to traverse the references manually, which introduces the very overhead you wanted to avoid by choosing MongoDB in the first place!

As of this writing, only half of the programming language drivers available provide support for DBRefs:

- Provides DBRef support: C#, Java, Node.js, Perl, Python, Ruby

- Does not provide DBRefs support: C, C++, Haskell, PHP, Scala

Embedded documents

A better data-modeling solution would be simply to collapse the normalized relationships and fold the related information into *embedded* (`https://docs.mongodb.com/manual/core/data-model-design/#data-modeling-embedding`) documents. Using the preceding example, the better solution would appear as follows:

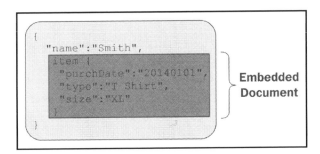

Using embedded documents, with a single query, you can easily obtain a consolidated block of information, which includes the customer name, purchase date, and specifics on the item.

MongoDB also supports creating indexes (`https://docs.mongodb.com/manual/indexes/`) on any given field, which boosts query performance. The auto-generated `_id` field is automatically indexed. It should be noted, however, that creating too many indexes will have a negative impact on performance when writing data.

Document design

When designing documents, which will ultimately end up in collections, one way to start off the design process would be to gain an understanding of what outputs (such as printed reports, or data that will be pulled up on a screen at some point). You can then work your way backwards to decide which documents need to be created. As an example, let's take the one shown just now: **customers**, **products**, and **purchases**.

If at some point you need to print a customer report, it might be appropriate to design a customer collection. You should only include information that needs to go into the report. In a like manner, you might have an inventory of products that need to be tracked. You would then design a product collection, including only the information which needs to appear in the report or on a screen display:

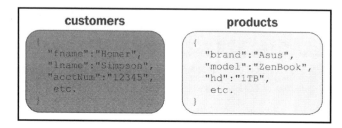

When we get to purchases, it gets a little tricky. Probably the most difficult aspect of document design is to shake off your SQL viewpoint, if that is your background. The SQL way of doing things would be to design a minimal purchase document, and have a reference to the associated customer and product documents. As mentioned previously, this would introduce tremendous difficulties when it comes time to querying and producing any output. A more expedient design would be simply to embed the associated documents inside the purchase document:

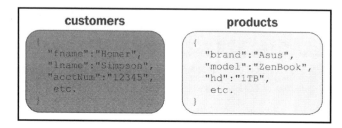

Another situation where SQL-based thinking will not serve you well is when you want to implement a series of lookup tables. For example, let's say you want to populate an HTML SELECT form element from a database. As an example, let's assume the first select element gives users a choice of social media; Facebook, Twitter, Instagram, and so on. The other select element consists of a list of categories; Shirts, Blouses, Jeans, Jackets, Footwear, and so on.

If you are thinking in SQL terms, you would probably create a table for each type, and then have a single row for each item. As an example, you might have a table called social_media with the two columns id and type, where type would be Facebook, Twitter, and so on:

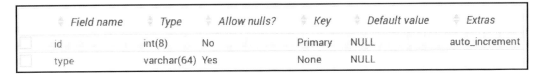

Field name	Type	Allow nulls?	Key	Default value	Extras
id	int(8)	No	Primary	NULL	auto_increment
type	varchar(64)	Yes	None	NULL	

You would then create a table categories, again with the two columns id and category, where category would be Shirts, Blouses, and so on:

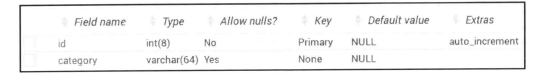

Field name	Type	Allow nulls?	Key	Default value	Extras
id	int(8)	No	Primary	NULL	auto_increment
category	varchar(64)	Yes	None	NULL	

To do the same thing in MongoDB, you might create a collection called select_options, with two documents. The first document would have a field type, with a value Social Media. A second field would be an array that includes Facebook, Twitter, and so on. The second document would also have a field type with a value Categories.

The second field would be an array with `Shirts`, `Blouses`, and so on:

```
_id: ObjectId("5b2336da57b3f5706643ad8a")
type: "Social Media"
options: Array
    0: "Facebook"
    1: "Twitter"
    2: "Instagram"




_id: ObjectId("5b23382b57b3f5706643ad8b")
type: "Categories"
options: Array
    0: "Shirts"
    1: "Blouses"
    2: "Trousers"
    3: "etc."
```

 Any time you find yourself creating a large set of small documents, consider collapsing the collection into a single document with an embedded array. A good overview of data design is found here: `https://docs.mongodb.com/manual/core/data-model-design/`.

Creating a MongoDB database and collection

It is now time to put into practice how to create a MongoDB database and collection. The `Chapter 3`, *Using the MongoDB Shell*, will show you how to perform operations using the MongoDB shell. For the purposes of this introductory chapter we will use MongoDB Compass (`https://www.mongodb.com/products/compass`), which is a free graphical utility you can use to perform administration.

To create a MongoDB database and start a collection using MongoDB Compass, proceed as follows:

1. Open MongoDB Compass using the link as appropriate to your operating system. In this illustration we are using Ubuntu Linux, so we launch using the GUI.
2. Click on the plus sign (+) to create a database:

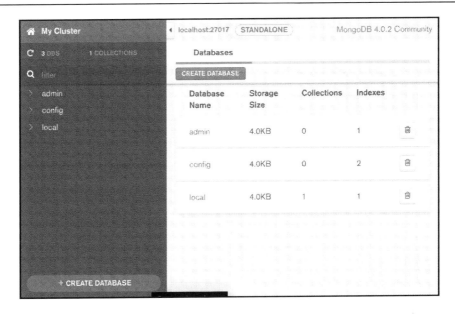

3. When the **Create Database** dialog box appears, enter the name of the database and the name of the first collection. When first creating a database, you cannot have one without the other. For this illustration, the database will be `sweetscomplete` and the first collection will be `customers`:

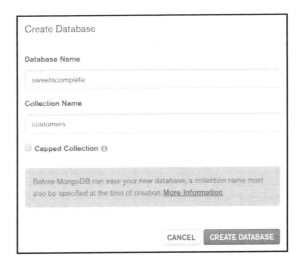

Congratulations! The database has now been created! If you click on its name in MongoDB Compass, you will see the newly created collection as well:

Consider jumping ahead to the *Simple Backup and Restore* topic in `Chapter 6`, *Maintaining MongoDB Performance*, in this book for a discussion on how to restore data. In the source code repository for this book, you will find a backup of sample data used in subsequent examples.

Summary

In this chapter, you learned:

- The architectural underpinnings of *NoSQL* databases and MongoDB, in particular
- MongoDB terms, including databases, collections, documents, and fields
- Data-modeling considerations, document design, and how to avoid SQL-based thinking
- How to create a MongoDB database and start a collection using MongoDB Compass

The next chapter will cover how to use the MongoDB shell to manage the database, including basic CRUD operations.

3
Using the MongoDB Shell

This chapter covers how to use the `mongo` (`https://docs.mongodb.com/manual/reference/program/mongo/#bin.mongo`) command shell to perform simple **CRUD (Create, Read, Update, and Delete)** operations on the database. In addition, you'll learn how to customize the shell and run scripts directly from the command line. This chapter will be of critical interest to DBAs (database admins), but also developers and IT professionals who want to know what is possible.

The topics that we will learn in this chapter are:

- Overview
- Performing Simple Queries
- Database and Collection Operations
- Creating, Updating, or Deleting Documents
- Creating and Running Shell Scripts

Overview

The `mongo` is an executable installed as part of MongoDB. When run, this utility provides an interactive JavaScript command line style interface to the MongoDB database. You can use the shell to perform any and all actions on the MongoDB database including queries, adding, editing, and removing documents from collections. You can also perform higher level operations such as creating a database and collections.

Why use the mongo shell?

A fair question to ask is *why use the mongo shell*? After all, given that the wonderful graphical utility *MongoDB Compass* is provided free-of-charge, why bother with the shell? The answer lies in the very nature of *Compass*; it's *graphical* in nature, which means you are out of luck when a customer in another city (or even another country!) calls you late on a Friday to tell you the database is down.

Although *Compass* can connect remotely, its requirements are much more demanding, and you would most likely need the support of the customer IT department to successfully connect. The mongo shell, on the other hand, is text based and only requires a simple, relatively common SSH connection to a server on the customer site.

Another massive advantage of the mongo shell over *Compass* is that the shell can run scripts. Getting back to the late Friday Emergency scenario, imagine being able to upload and run a *rescue* script over an SSH connection, rather than trying to perform manual surgery on the customer's database using *Compass*.

Options when invoking the shell

Here are some common command line options (`https://docs.mongodb.com/manual/reference/program/mongo/#options`) when invoking mongo:

- `mongo`: Opens up the interactive command shell.
- `mongo -u username -p password -h host --port nnnn --ssl`: The first two options are needed when security has been configured. The next two options are needed when accessing a remote MongoDB instance. The last option secures the command stream using TLS or SSL. Also, refer to the Chapter 7, *Securing MongoDB*, in this book for more information on setting up TLS/SSL.
- `mongo some_JavaScript_file.js`: Executes a JavaScript file containing MongoDB commands.
- `mongo --eval 'JavaScript'`: Directly runs the JavaScript commands in quotes.
- `mongo --help`: Get help on using the mongo command shell.
- `exit`: Invokes `quit()`, which closes the shell returning you to the command line.

The `mongo` command line options shown here can be combined. As an example, to run a script `abc.js` on a remote MongoDB server `remote.mongo.com`, as user `fred` and with a password of `flintstone`, the command might appear as follows:

```
mongo abc.js -h remote.mongo.com -u fred -p flintstone
```

Before you invoke the shell, it is *extremely important* to make sure the MongoDB database is up and running! If, after running the `mongo` command you see a message similar to this, the database instance is probably not running:

```
$ mongo
MongoDB shell version v4.0.0
connecting to: mongodb://127.0.0.1:27017
2018-07-04T10:41:29.866+0700 E QUERY     [js] Error:
couldn't connect to server 127.0.0.1:27017, connection
attempt failed: SocketException: Error connecting to
127.0.0.1:27017 :: caused by :: Connection refused :
connect@src/mongo/shell/mongo.js:251:13
@(connect):1:6
exception: connect failed
```

.mongorc.js File

All command line option flags can be coded into a file, `mongorc.js` (`https://docs.mongodb.com/manual/reference/program/mongo/#files`). When you run the `mongo` command, this file is parsed unless you include the command line switch `mongo --norc`. There are two primary locations for this file; the user home directory, or the operating system's `/etc` directory:

```
fred@fred-linux:~$ ls -l .mongorc.js
-rw------- 1 fred fred 42 Jun 26 11:03 .mongorc.js
fred@fred-linux:~$ ls -l /etc/mongorc.js
-rwxr-xr-x 1 mongodb root 42 Jun 26 11:04 /etc/mongorc.js
fred@fred-linux:~$ █
```

It is very important to set the rights properly if using `/etc/mongorc.js`. Otherwise, you will receive a permissions error when the `mongo` shell first starts. The recommended rights would be to assign ownership to the user `mongodb`, and `read` + `execute` rights to all others.

Here is a sample `mongorc.js` file, which customizes the prompt (`https://docs.mongodb.com/manual/tutorial/configure-mongo-shell/`) to display the database, hostname, and up time:

```
.mongorc.js ✖
host = db.serverStatus().host;
upTime = db.serverStatus().uptime;
prompt = function() {
    return db+"@"+host+"[up:"+upTime+"]> ";
}
```

If you have defined *both* a global `/etc/mongorc.js` as well as a `~/.mongorc.js` config file in the user home folder, the global file will be processed first. Another important consideration is that if the user uses the `--norc` option, it only suppresses execution of the local home directory file, not the global `mongorc.js` file.

Informational commands

There is a series of useful commands, referred to as *command helpers* (`https://docs.mongodb.com/manual/reference/mongo-shell/#command-helpers`), that is available from inside the shell. Once you are in the shell, simply type `help`, and you will see the help quick reference, shown here:

```
> help
        db.help()                    help on db methods
        db.mycoll.help()             help on collection methods
        sh.help()                    sharding helpers
        rs.help()                    replica set helpers
        help admin                   administrative help
        help connect                 connecting to a db help
        help keys                    key shortcuts
        help misc                    misc things to know
        help mr                      mapreduce

        show dbs                     show database names
        show collections            show collections in current database
        show users                   show users in current database
        show profile                 show most recent system.profile entries with time >= 1ms
        show logs                    show the accessible logger names
        show log [name]              prints out the last segment of log in memory, 'global' is default
        use <db_name>                set current database
        db.foo.find()                list objects in collection foo
        db.foo.find( { a : 1 } )     list objects in foo where a == 1
        it                           result of the last line evaluated; use to further iterate
        DBQuery.shellBatchSize = x   set default number of items to display on shell
        exit                         quit the mongo shell
```

The `mongo` shell enables most of the common keystroke editing shortcuts (`https://docs.mongodb.com/manual/reference/mongo-shell/#keyboard-shortcuts`) available in most text editors (for example, Windows *Notepad*, or Linux *gedit*). Accordingly, you can use *home* and *end* to move to the beginning and end of the current line, and so on. In addition, the shell maintains a *history*. The *up* and *down* arrows move through previously entered commands.

Performing simple queries

Command summary (discussed as follows):

- `db.<collection>.find({<filter>},{<projection>}).<aggregation>()` : Returns only one or more documents based on the filter expression. The projection expression includes or excludes document fields. Aggregation is used to manipulate the final result set (for example, `sort()`, `limit()`, and so on).

- `db.<collection>.findOne({<filter>},{<projection>})`: Returns only one document based on the filter expression. The projection expression includes or excludes document fields.

One of the most common operations on any database is *querying* the database for information, which will then form the basis of reports and information that might appear on a web page. In MongoDB the primary command to perform a query is `db.<collection>.find()`. There is also a variation `db.<collection>.findOne()`, which only returns a single result.

For those who are used to SQL parlance, the term *query* can also be used to describe any SQL statement sent to the RDBMS. In the MongoDB documentation, the term *query* is used in conjunction with performing a `find` operation.

The `find()` (https://docs.mongodb.com/manual/reference/command/find/#find) command takes optional two arguments, *filter* and *projection* (https://docs.mongodb.com/manual/reference/glossary/#term-projection). If you do not specify any arguments, `find()` returns all documents in the collection:

```
sweetscomplete@fred-linux[up:174546]> db.products.find();
{ "_id" : ObjectId("5b34651536adf7141a398f73"), "sku" : "F1000", "title" : "Fudge", "description" : "Invenire percipitur eum ea, in saepe per", "price" : "0.10" }
{ "_id" : ObjectId("5b34651536adf7141a398f74"), "sku" : "S2000", "title" : "Sugar Cookies", "description" : "Ei vix patrioque similique referrentur, ", "price" : "0.20"
}
{ "_id" : ObjectId("5b34651536adf7141a398f75"), "sku" : "C3000", "title" : "Chocolate Angelfood Cupcakes", "description" : "Id ius detracto constituam, his possit p", "p
rice" : "0.30" }
{ "_id" : ObjectId("5b34651536adf7141a398f76"), "sku" : "P4000", "title" : "Peanut Brittle", "description" : "Aliquam maiestatis mea eu. Vel quot rebu", "price" : "0.40"
}
{ "_id" : ObjectId("5b34651536adf7141a398f77"), "sku" : "T5000", "title" : "Toasted Marshmallows", "description" : "Ne mea velit tation euismod. Nec ludico ", "price" :
"0.50" }
{ "_id" : ObjectId("5b34651536adf7141a398f78"), "sku" : "F6000", "title" : "Fruit Salad", "description" : "Vis quem voluptatum in. Id magna inimicu", "price" : "0.60" }
{ "_id" : ObjectId("5b34651536adf7141a398f79"), "sku" : "C7000", "title" : "Cheesecake", "description" : "Munere irure tamquam no quo, sit ei tam", "price" : "0.70" }
{ "_id" : ObjectId("5b34651536adf7141a398f7a"), "sku" : "G8000", "title" : "Glazed Doughnut", "description" : "Mel wisi decore habemus ad, et his debit", "price" : "0.80
}
{ "_id" : ObjectId("5b34651536adf7141a398f7b"), "sku" : "F9000", "title" : "Fortune Cookies", "description" : "Oratio pericula sapientem te eum. Mei tr", "price" : "0.90
00" }
{ "_id" : ObjectId("5b34651536adf7141a398f7c"), "sku" : "D10000", "title" : "Devils Food Cake", "description" : "Ius nulla phaedrum ex, aliquip ullamcorp", "price" : "1.
00" }
{ "_id" : ObjectId("5b34651536adf7141a398f7d"), "sku" : "P11000", "title" : "Peanut Butter Cups", "description" : "Vim et patrioque adolescens. Ludus ubiqu", "price" : "
1.10" }
{ "_id" : ObjectId("5b34651536adf7141a398f7e"), "sku" : "C12000", "title" : "Crispy Rice Treats", "description" : "Cu inani nonumy vituperatoribus nec, ut ", "price" : "
1.20" }
{ "_id" : ObjectId("5b34651536adf7141a398f7f"), "sku" : "C13000", "title" : "Cherry Pie", "description" : "Putant volumus reformidans in pri. Per e", "price" : "1.30" }
{ "_id" : ObjectId("5b34651536adf7141a398f80"), "sku" : "A14000", "title" : "Apple Turnover", "description" : "Vel id sumo assum, possim consequuntur s", "price" : "1.40
}
{ "_id" : ObjectId("5b34651536adf7141a398f81"), "sku" : "N15000", "title" : "Napoleon", "description" : "Sed an agam nominati, eam ubique ornatus", "price" : "1.50" }
{ "_id" : ObjectId("5b34651536adf7141a398f82"), "sku" : "C16000", "title" : "Chocolate Chip Cookies", "description" : "Vel sonet audire ea, no latine scriptore", "price"
: "1.60" }
{ "_id" : ObjectId("5b34651536adf7141a398f83"), "sku" : "C17000", "title" : "Chocolate Soufflé", "description" : "Quo oratio aperiri officiis te. Vel elit", "price" : "1
.70" }
{ "_id" : ObjectId("5b34651536adf7141a398f84"), "sku" : "W18000", "title" : "Walnut Brownies", "description" : "Sanctus ocurreret eloquentiam ad qui, ut", "price" : "1.8
0" }
{ "_id" : ObjectId("5b34651536adf7141a398f85"), "sku" : "A19000", "title" : "Ambrosia Salad", "description" : "Oblique vivendo legendos an vel. Has ne ", "price" : "1.90
}
{ "_id" : ObjectId("5b34651536adf7141a398f86"), "sku" : "P20000", "title" : "Peach Cobbler", "description" : "Et consul nostrum copiosae duo, usu cibo", "price" : "2.00" }
Type "it" for more.
```

It's important to note the return value from `find()` is not the actual result set itself, rather what the MongoDB documentation calls a *cursor* (https://docs.mongodb.com/manual/tutorial/iterate-a-cursor/#iterate-a-cursor-in-the-mongo-shell). This is an iteration, a resource pointer, which can then be used to extract results. The command shell will automatically iterate the cursor 20 times (default), so there is no need for extra logic. If there are more than 20 results, you will be prompted:

```
Type "it" for more.
```

Aggregation (https://docs.mongodb.com/manual/aggregation/) or *cursor modifier* is the MongoDB term used to describe additional treatment of the cursor result. Examples covered in this chapter are limited to the *single purpose* (https://docs.mongodb.com/manual/aggregation/#single-purpose-aggregation-operations) aggregation operators `sort()` and `limit()`.

For information on how to define more complex forms of aggregation (for example, cursor manipulation) including *pipelines* and *map-reduce*, please refer `Chapter 5`, *Building Complex Queries Using Aggregation*, in this book.

Defining a query filter

The *filter* (`https://docs.mongodb.com/manual/tutorial/query-documents/`) is a JSON expression, which defines criteria by which documents are either included in or excluded from the final result set. The filter usually consists of two elements, a document field name and an expression. The expression can be a hard-coded value, a *regular expression* (`https://en.wikipedia.org/wiki/Regular_expression`), or a statement that involves one or more query selectors (`https://docs.mongodb.com/manual/reference/operator/query/#query-selectors`) (or operators).

A brief list of built-in query selectors is shown here:

Operator	Meaning	Operator	Meaning
`$eq`	equal to	`$and`	logical AND
`$ne`	not equal to	`$or`	logical OR
`$lt`	less than	`$not`	logical NOT
`$lte`	less than or equal to	`$exists`	true if document has this field
`$gt`	greater than	`/regex/modifier`	any regular expression/modifier
`$gte`	greater than or equal to		
`$in`	in (followed by an array of values)		
`$nin`	not in (array of values)		

 In addition to the comparison and logical operators listed previously, MongoDB includes a rich set of additional expression operator categories (`https://docs.mongodb.com/manual/meta/aggregation-quick-reference/#operator-expressions`); arithmetic, array, Boolean, conditional, date, literal, object, set, string, text, types, accumulators, and variable expressions.

In the example shown here, we query the `products` collection in the `sweetscomplete` database. The query specifies that the field `price` should be greater than two and less than eight. In addition, the field `title` must include the word `chocolate` (using a case insensitive regular expression). Finally, the results are sorted by the field `sku`:

```
sweetscomplete@fred-linux[up:256884]> db.products.find(                    Collection
...      {
...              price:{$gt:"2",$lt:"8"},
...              title:/chocolate/i                                         Query
...      },
...      {                                                                  Projection
...              _id:0,description:0
...      }
...  ).sort({sku:1});                                                       Cursor Modifier
{ "sku" :  "C21000", "title" : "Chocolate Eclair", "price" : "2.10" }
{ "sku" : "C22000", "title" : "Chocolate Toaster Tarts", "price" : "2.20" }
{ "sku" : "C30000", "title" : "Chocolate Mousse", "price" : "3.00" }
{ "sku" : "C32000", "title" : "Chocolate Fondue", "price" : "3.20" }
{ "sku" : "C61000", "title" : "Chocolate Layer Cake", "price" : "6.10" }
{ "sku" : "M43000", "title" : "Mint Chocolate Milk Shake", "price" : "4.30" }
sweetscomplete@fred-linux[up:256884]>
```

You will also note that a *projection* (discussed next) is used to remove the fields `_id` and `description` from the final output.

Defining a projection

The *projection* delineates which fields within a document are included in or excluded from the final output. In MongoDB, the projection takes the form of a JSON expression consisting of `key:value` pairs. The key is the name of the field, and the value is either 1 or 0. Fields to be included are assigned 1. Fields to be excluded are assigned 0. By default, all fields are included.

For this illustration, assume a collection `products` where each document has the fields `_id`, `sku`, `title`, `price`, and `description`. We start by searching for all documents that have *Cookies* in the title, and only want to see `sku`, `title`, and `price`. Your initial thought might be to issue a `find()` where the projection is; `{sku:1,title:1,price:1}`:

```
sweetscomplete@fred-linux[up:451235]> db.products.find({title:/Cookies/},{sku:1,title:1,price:1});
{ "_id" : ObjectId("5b34651536adf7141a398f74"), "sku" : "S2000", "title" : "Sugar Cookies", "price" : "0.20" }
{ "_id" : ObjectId("5b34651536adf7141a398f7b"), "sku" : "F9000", "title" : "Fortune Cookies", "price" : "0.90" }
{ "_id" : ObjectId("5b34651536adf7141a398f82"), "sku" : "C16000", "title" : "Chocolate Chip Cookies", "price" : "1.60" }
{ "_id" : ObjectId("5b34653d36adf7141a398f8e"), "sku" : "P28000", "title" : "Peanut Butter Cookies", "price" : "2.80" }
{ "_id" : ObjectId("5b34653d36adf7141a398f8f"), "sku" : "029000", "title" : "Oatmeal Raisin Cookies", "price" : "2.90" }
{ "_id" : ObjectId("5b34653d36adf7141a398f97"), "sku" : "G37000", "title" : "Gingerbread Cookies", "price" : "3.70" }
{ "_id" : ObjectId("5b34654a36adf7141a398fb0"), "sku" : "S62000", "title" : "Shortbread Cookies", "price" : "6.20" }
{ "_id" : ObjectId("5b34654a36adf7141a398fb1"), "sku" : "063000", "title" : "Oreo Cookies", "price" : "6.30" }
sweetscomplete@fred-linux[up:451235]>
```

You can see, however, that the auto-generated `ObjectId` field is automatically included. To suppress, add `_id:0` to the preceding list, so you have:
`db.products.find({title:/Cookies/},{_id:0,sku:1,title:1,price:1}); :`

```
sweetscomplete@fred-linux[up:539431]>  db.products.find({title:/Cookies/},{_id:0,sku:1,title:1,price:1});
{ "sku" : "S2000", "title" : "Sugar Cookies", "price" : "0.20" }
{ "sku" : "F9000", "title" : "Fortune Cookies", "price" : "0.90" }
{ "sku" : "C16000", "title" : "Chocolate Chip Cookies", "price" : "1.60" }
{ "sku" : "P28000", "title" : "Peanut Butter Cookies", "price" : "2.80" }
{ "sku" : "O29000", "title" : "Oatmeal Raisin Cookies", "price" : "2.90" }
{ "sku" : "G37000", "title" : "Gingerbread Cookies", "price" : "3.70" }
{ "sku" : "S62000", "title" : "Shortbread Cookies", "price" : "6.20" }
{ "sku" : "O63000", "title" : "Oreo Cookies", "price" : "6.30" }
sweetscomplete@fred-linux[up:539431]>
```

Alternatively, you can simply suppress `_id` and `description` to achieve exactly the same results:

```
sweetscomplete@fred-linux[up:539431]> db.products.find({title:/Cookies/},{_id:0,description:0});
{ "sku" : "S2000", "title" : "Sugar Cookies", "price" : "0.20" }
{ "sku" : "F9000", "title" : "Fortune Cookies", "price" : "0.90" }
{ "sku" : "C16000", "title" : "Chocolate Chip Cookies", "price" : "1.60" }
{ "sku" : "P28000", "title" : "Peanut Butter Cookies", "price" : "2.80" }
{ "sku" : "O29000", "title" : "Oatmeal Raisin Cookies", "price" : "2.90" }
{ "sku" : "G37000", "title" : "Gingerbread Cookies", "price" : "3.70" }
{ "sku" : "S62000", "title" : "Shortbread Cookies", "price" : "6.20" }
{ "sku" : "O63000", "title" : "Oreo Cookies", "price" : "6.30" }
sweetscomplete@fred-linux[up:539431]> █
```

Modifying the cursor

To have the results appear in a certain order and/or limit the number of results, we introduce the simple cursor modifiers `sort()` and `limit()`. These can be stacked as each method returns the cursor. Much like a projection, `sort()` takes a JSON expression as an argument, with key:value pairs to form the sort criteria. The field that influences the sort is the key, and the value can be 1 for ascending, and −1 for descending. If you want to have multiple fields represented, just add the additional fields using a comma to separate the pairs.

In this example, you can see that the field `price` is used as the sort criterion, ascending order. This is followed by an identical command where the order is descending:

```
Ascending Sort
>db.products.find({},{_id:0,description:0}).sort({price:1}).limit(5);
{ "sku" : "F1000", "title" : "Fudge", "price" : "0.10" }
{ "sku" : "S2000", "title" : "Sugar Cookies", "price" : "0.20" }
{ "sku" : "C3000", "title" : "Chocolate Angelfood Cupcakes", "price" : "0.30" }
{ "sku" : "P4000", "title" : "Peanut Brittle", "price" : "0.40" }
{ "sku" : "T5000", "title" : "Toasted Marshmallows", "price" : "0.50" }
>
Descending Sort
>db.products.find({},{_id:0,description:0}).sort({price:-1}).limit(5);
{ "sku" : "P64000", "title" : "Pop Tarts", "price" : "6.40" }
{ "sku" : "O63000", "title" : "Oreo Cookies", "price" : "6.30" }
{ "sku" : "S62000", "title" : "Shortbread Cookies", "price" : "6.20" }
{ "sku" : "C61000", "title" : "Chocolate Layer Cake", "price" : "6.10" }
{ "sku" : "B60000", "title" : "Banana Bread", "price" : "6.00" }
>
```

Database and collection operations

Occasionally, you may find yourself in the position where you need to do quick edits on the *database*. As we mentioned, you can often use the GUI tool *MongoDB Compass*, however there may be times when you are limited an SSH connection and command line access. The best word of advice we can give you at this point is to brush up on your JavaScript! In this sub-section we will cover creating and dropping databases and collections.

Working with databases

Command summary (discussed in the following):

- Create a Database:

```
use <dbName>;
db.<collection>.insertOne({ // document });
```

- Drop a Database:

```
use <dbName>;
db.dropDatabase();
```

To create a database in MongoDB, all you need to do is to issue the command `use dbName`, where `dbName` is the name of the target database. This alone does not create the database. As shown here when creating the database `test`, although the customized prompt (see the previous) shows the current database is `test`, when the command `show dbs` is executed, `test` does not appear in the list:

```
local@fred-linux[up:85273]> use test;
switched to db test
test@fred-linux[up:85273]> show dbs;
admin                 0.000GB
config                0.000GB
local                 0.000GB
mongodb_quickstart    0.000GB
sweetscomplete        0.000GB
test@fred-linux[up:85273]>
```

Once you create the first document, in the first collection, however, the database will appear. In the example shown, we create a collection `users`:

```
test@fred-linux[up:85273]> db.users.insertOne({ firstName: "Fred",lastName: "Flintstone",status: "Cave Man"});
{
        "acknowledged" : true,
        "insertedId" : ObjectId("5b330bc44a8f38b62dcff69d")
}
test@fred-linux[up:85273]> show dbs;
admin                 0.000GB
config                0.000GB
local                 0.000GB
mongodb_quickstart    0.000GB
sweetscomplete        0.000GB
test                  0.000GB
test@fred-linux[up:85273]>
```

To drop the database, first `use` the database, and then issue the command `db.dropDatabase()` as shown here. You will note that the database `test` is no longer shown when the `show dbs` command is issued:

```
test@fred-linux[up:85273]> use test;
switched to db test
test@fred-linux[up:85273]> db.dropDatabase();
{ "dropped" : "test", "ok" : 1 }
test@fred-linux[up:85273]> show dbs;
admin                 0.000GB
config                0.000GB
local                 0.000GB
mongodb_quickstart    0.000GB
sweetscomplete        0.000GB
test@fred-linux[up:85273]>
```

Working with collections

Command summary (discussed in the following):

- Create a Collection:

```
use <dbName>;
db.<collection>.insertOne({ // document });
or
db.createCollection(<collection>);
```

- Delete a Collection:

```
use <dbName>;
db.<collection>.drop();
```

The procedure for creating a new collection is identical to the one discussed previously when creating a new database. You first use the database, and then use either of the db.<collection> methods insertOne() or insertMany() to add one or more documents. Alternatively, you can use the db.createCollection() method to create an empty collection. The command show collections shows you which collections have been defined for this database:

```
test@fred-linux[up:85273]> use test;
switched to db test
test@fred-linux[up:85273]> db.products.insertOne({ title: "Hammer",price: 99.99});
{
        "acknowledged" : true,
        "insertedId" : ObjectId("5b3311e64a8f38b62dcff6a2")
}
test@fred-linux[up:85273]> db.createCollection("users");
{ "ok" : 1 }
test@fred-linux[up:85273]> show collections;
products
users
test@fred-linux[up:85273]> ▮
```

To remove the collection, simply issue the command `db.<collection>.drop()`, where `collection` is the name of the collection to be removed from that database:

```
test@fred-linux[up:85273]> show collections;
products
users
test@fred-linux[up:85273]> db.users.drop();
true
test@fred-linux[up:85273]> show collections;
products
test@fred-linux[up:85273]> █
```

Creating, updating, or deleting documents

In MongoDB, the *document* is the lowest atomic unit that can be addressed. As mentioned in Chapter 2, *Understanding MongoDB Data Structures*, a document is a JSON expression that contains a set of `key:value` pairs. The `key` is the name of the field and the `value` is the actual data used to form the document.

The MongoDB API consistently provides methods for both single and multiple operations. The generic form is `(insert|update|delete)(One|Many)()`. So, for example, if you wish to insert many documents, use `insertMany()`. If you only wish to delete only one, use `deleteOne()`, and so forth.

Creating one or more documents

Command summary (discussed in the following):

- `db.<collection>.insertOne({ // document });`
- `db.<collection>.insertMany([{ // document },{ // document },etc.]);`

The main focus when using the `insertOne()` or `insertMany()` command is on the *document*. The document must be a well formed JSON expression. Document fields can contain arrays, or even other documents.

If you only wish to insert a single document use `insertOne()`. Here is an example where we insert a customer *Conrad Perry* into the `sweetscomplete` database, `customers` collection. Note that the unique identifier `ObjectId` is auto-generated:

```
>db.customers.insertOne(
... {
...     "name": "Conrad Perry",
...     "address": "79 Amber Branch Falls",
...     "city": "Birdseye",
...     "state_province": "QC",
...     "postal_code": "G0U 0M5",
...     "country": "CA",
...     "phone": "484-181-9811",
...     "balance": "745.32",
...     "email": "conrad.perry@fastmedia.com",
...     "password": "$2y$10$mSzJOY9uvWbkaYLPgG6uEeOMnbZf3LdC25cTkgpFT6ueWCnqW.Y1a"
... }
... );
{
        "acknowledged" : true,
        "insertedId" : ObjectId("5b39a2d31539fefbb18b04d7")
}
>
```

In this example we insert many documents, but only the fields `name` and `email`:

```
>db.customers.insertMany(
...     [
...         {"name":"Lonnie Knapp","email":"lonnie.knapp@cablecom.com"},
...         {"name":"Darrel Roman","email":"darrel.roman@southcom.net"},
...         {"name":"Morgan Avila","email":"morgan.avila@northmedia.com"},
...     ]
... );
{
        "acknowledged" : true,
        "insertedIds" : [
                ObjectId("5b39a53b1539fefbb18b04d8"),
                ObjectId("5b39a53b1539fefbb18b04d9"),
                ObjectId("5b39a53b1539fefbb18b04da")
        ]
}
>
```

If we then execute a `find()` you can see that even though the number of fields between documents in this collection are mismatched, MongoDB has no problem with this:

```
>db.customers.find().pretty();
{
        "_id" : ObjectId("5b39a2d31539fefbb18b04d7"),
        "name" : "Conrad Perry",
        "address" : "79 Amber Branch Falls",
        "city" : "Birdseye",
        "state_province" : "QC",
        "postal_code" : "G0U 0M5",
        "country" : "CA",
        "phone" : "484-181-9811",
        "balance" : "745.32",
        "email" : "conrad.perry@fastmedia.com",
        "password" : "$2y$10$mSzJOY9uvWbkaYLPgG6uEeOMnbZf3LdC25cTkgpFT6ueWCnqW.Y1a"
}
{
        "_id" : ObjectId("5b39a53b1539fefbb18b04d8"),
        "name" : "Lonnie Knapp",
        "email" : "lonnie.knapp@cablecom.com"
}
{
        "_id" : ObjectId("5b39a53b1539fefbb18b04d9"),
        "name" : "Darrel Roman",
        "email" : "darrel.roman@southcom.net"
}
{
        "_id" : ObjectId("5b39a53b1539fefbb18b04da"),
        "name" : "Morgan Avila",
        "email" : "morgan.avila@northmedia.com"
}
>
```

It is not mandatory that all documents have the same fields, or even the same number of fields. It is completely possible to create a collection that consists of a series of unrelated documents. Such an example might be to define the `key:value` pairs needed to present a form with radio buttons, checkboxes, and select elements.

If you need to run other commands in conjunction with each insert, consider using `bulkWrite()` (https://docs.mongodb.com/manual/reference/method/db.collection.bulkWrite/), which lets you specify an array of operations to be performed. This command can be used to perform multiple `*One()` operations with precise control over the order of execution.

Updating one or more documents

Command summary (discussed as follows):

- db.<collection>.updateOne({<filter>},{<update>}[,{upsert:true}]
  );
- db.<collection>.updateMany({<filter>},{<update>}[,{upsert:true}
  ]);
- db.<collection>.replaceOne({<filter>},{ // document
  }[,{upsert:true}]);

Both update*() and delete*() use a filter. The good news is that the filter uses exactly the same syntax as the find() command, mentioned previously. The difference between updateOne() and replaceOne() is that with the former you only need to supply the fields that need to be set or unset, whereas with the latter (for example, replaceOne()) you need to supply an entire replacement document. If the upsert parameter is set to true, a new document is inserted if the update or replace command fails to find a document that matches the filter.

In order to use either updateOne() or updateMany(), the first argument is a query filter. The second argument must use an *update operator* (https://docs.mongodb.com/manual/reference/operator/update/#update-operators). The syntax takes this form; { operator: { field: value, ... } }. Here is a partial list of operators:

- $inc: It is used to increment the value of an integer field.
- $set: It is used to assign a value. If the field is not present, adds this field to the documents.
- $unset: It removes the field from the document.
- $rename: It changes the name of a field.

In this example we update a customer Conrad Perry (shown in the preceding insert). We update his phone number from 484-181-9811 to 111-222-3333, and his account balance to 544.88:

```
>db.customers.updateOne(
...      { name:"Conrad Perry" },
...      { $set:
...          {
...              "phone" : "111-222-3333",
...              "balance" : 544.88
...          }
...      }
... );
{ "acknowledged" : true, "matchedCount" : 1, "modifiedCount" : 1 }
>
>db.customers.find({name:"Conrad Perry"},{name:1,phone:1,balance:1}).pretty();
{
        "_id" : ObjectId("5b39a2d31539fefbb18b04d7"),
        "name" : "Conrad Perry",
        "phone" : "111-222-3333",
        "balance" : 544.88
}
>
```

In the next example we add a field `balance` to customers `Lonnie Knapp`, `Darrel Roman`, and `Morgan Avila`:

```
>db.customers.updateMany(
...      { name: { $in: ["Lonnie Knapp", "Darrel Roman", "Morgan Avila"] }},
...      { $set: { "balance" : 0.0 } }
... );
{ "acknowledged" : true, "matchedCount" : 3, "modifiedCount" : 3 }
>
>db.customers.find({},{name:1,phone:1,balance:1}).pretty();
{
        "_id" : ObjectId("5b39a2d31539fefbb18b04d7"),
        "name" : "Conrad Perry",
        "phone" : "111-222-3333",
        "balance" : 544.88
}
{
        "_id" : ObjectId("5b39a53b1539fefbb18b04d8"),
        "name" : "Lonnie Knapp",
        "balance" : 0
}
{
        "_id" : ObjectId("5b39a53b1539fefbb18b04d9"),
        "name" : "Darrel Roman",
        "balance" : 0
}
{
        "_id" : ObjectId("5b39a53b1539fefbb18b04da"),
        "name" : "Morgan Avila",
        "balance" : 0
}
>
```

And in our last example in this sub-section, we use `replaceOne()` to replace a customer Lee Mccray. This user does not exist in this collection. Because the `upsert` parameter was set to `true`, however, MongoDB performs an insert instead:

```
>db.customers.replaceOne(
...     { name: "Lee Mccray" },
...     {
...         "name" : "Lee Mccray",
...         "address" : "195 Grand Dale Acres",
...         "city" : "Cake",
...         "state_province" : "QC",
...         "postal_code" : "DD65 82QD",
...         "country" : "UK",
...         "phone" : "265-666-2636",
...         "balance" : 539.35,
...         "email" : "lee.mccray@southnet.com",
...         "password" : "new5220and"
...     },
...     { upsert: true }
... );
{
        "acknowledged" : true,
        "matchedCount" : 0,
        "modifiedCount" : 0,
        "upsertedId" : ObjectId("5b39dbfa631cd39f250ea2bf")
}
>
```

We definitely **do not** want to store his password as plain text, however, so we follow that with an `updateOne()` command instructing MongoDB to remove this field (presumably to be added later with proper hashing):

```
>db.customers.updateOne(
...     { name: "Lee Mccray" },
...     { $unset: { "password" : 1 } }
... );
{ "acknowledged" : true, "matchedCount" : 1, "modifiedCount" : 1 }
>
```

We then issue a simple `find()` command to make sure the document is correct:

```
>db.customers.find({ name: "Lee Mccray" }).pretty();
{
        "_id" : ObjectId("5b39dbfa631cd39f250ea2bf"),
        "name" : "Lee Mccray",
        "address" : "195 Grand Dale Acres",
        "city" : "Cake",
        "state_province" : "QC",
        "postal_code" : "DD65 82QD",
        "country" : "UK",
        "phone" : "265-666-2636",
        "balance" : 539.35,
        "email" : "lee.mccray@southnet.com"
}
>
```

Even though `replaceOne()` completely replaces the old document with the new one, it retains the old `ObjectId` (`_id`) field.

Deleting one or more documents

Command summary (discussed as follows):

- db.<collection>.deleteOne({<filter>});
- db.<collection>.deleteMany({<filter>});

As you can see from the command summary, the main focus of `delete*()` commands is the *filter*. You use the same syntax as you would when executing `find()`. Because the `delete*()` commands can potentially delete all data from a collection if you make a mistake in the filter, it is recommended you use `deleteOne()` whenever possible.

In this example we delete a customer with the name `C. T. Russell`:

```
>db.customers.deleteOne({"name":"C.T. Russell"});
{ "acknowledged" : true, "deletedCount" : 1 }
>
```

Before you execute `deleteMany()`, first run `find()` to see if the filter you're using yields the correct results. In this case we plan to delete all documents where the `password` field does not exist:

```
>db.customers.find({password:{$exists:0}},{name:1,email:1});
{ "_id" : ObjectId("5b39a53b1539fefbb18b04d8"), "name" : "Lonnie Knapp", "email" : "lonnie.knapp@cablecom.com" }
{ "_id" : ObjectId("5b39a53b1539fefbb18b04d9"), "name" : "Darrel Roman", "email" : "darrel.roman@southcom.net" }
{ "_id" : ObjectId("5b39a53b1539fefbb18b04da"), "name" : "Morgan Avila", "email" : "morgan.avila@northmedia.com" }
{ "_id" : ObjectId("5b39dbfa631cd39f250ea2bf"), "name" : "Lee Mccray", "email" : "lee.mccray@southnet.com" }
{ "_id" : ObjectId("5b39efbf1bd9ed476f570286"), "name" : "Karyn Francis", "email" : "karyn.francis@fastnet.com" }
{ "_id" : ObjectId("5b39efbf1bd9ed476f570287"), "name" : "Blanca Le", "email" : "blanca.le@telecom.com" }
{ "_id" : ObjectId("5b39efbf1bd9ed476f570288"), "name" : "Renee Decker", "email" : "renee.decker@westcom.net" }
{ "_id" : ObjectId("5b39efbf1bd9ed476f570289"), "name" : "Obama", "email" : "obama@president.gov" }
{ "_id" : ObjectId("5b39efbf1bd9ed476f57028a"), "name" : "C.T. Russell", "email" : "ctrussell@jw.org" }
>
```

Having verified that these are the documents we wish to target, we proceed with the delete operation using the same filter:

```
>db.customers.deleteMany({ "password" : { $exists : false } });
{ "acknowledged" : true, "deletedCount" : 9 }
>
```

Creating and running shell scripts

Command summary (discussed as follows):

- `mongo [<database>] --eval "command"`: Direct command execution
- `mongo <JavaScript>`: Runs the shell script specified

There are two ways in which you can run a shell script using `mongo`; issuing a direct (single) command using the `--eval` flag, or by creating and running a shell script.

Running a direct command

Often, you simply want to get status information on MongoDB, in which case the database is irrelevant. In this example, we use the `--eval` flag to run the command `db.serverStatus()`:

```
fred@fred-linux:~$ mongo --eval "db.serverStatus();"
MongoDB shell version v4.0.0
connecting to: mongodb://127.0.0.1:27017
MongoDB server version: 4.0.0
{
        "host" : "fred-linux",
        "version" : "4.0.0",
        "process" : "mongod",
        "pid" : NumberLong(15054),
        "uptime" : 828,
        "uptimeMillis" : NumberLong(828147),
        "uptimeEstimate" : NumberLong(828),
        "localTime" : ISODate("2018-07-04T03:58:28.386Z"),
```

In other cases, you might want to run periodic database queries from a *cron* job. Here is an example where we check for customers in the sweetscomplete database whose balance is 0:

```
fred@fred-linux:~$ mongo sweetscomplete --eval "db.customers.find
> (
>       {balance:0},
>       {name:1,email:1,balance:1}
> ).pretty();"
MongoDB shell version v4.0.0
connecting to: mongodb://127.0.0.1:27017/sweetscomplete
MongoDB server version: 4.0.0
{
        "_id" : ObjectId("5b3c4734f5a48120315c7167"),
        "name" : "Lonnie Knapp",
        "balance" : 0,
        "email" : "lonnie.knapp@cablecom.com"
}
{
        "_id" : ObjectId("5b3c4734f5a48120315c7168"),
        "name" : "Darrel Roman",
        "balance" : 0,
        "email" : "darrel.roman@southcom.net"
}
{
        "_id" : ObjectId("5b3c4734f5a48120315c7169"),
        "name" : "Morgan Avila",
        "balance" : 0,
        "email" : "morgan.avila@northmedia.com"
}
fred@fred-linux:~$ █
```

Running a shell script

The shell scripts you create and plan to run using the mongo shell must follow standard JavaScript (`https://developer.mozilla.org/en-US/docs/Web/JavaScript`) syntax. You are free to use any of the built-in mongo shell methods (`https://docs.mongodb.com/manual/reference/method/#mongo-shell-methods`), however the `mongo` command helpers (`https://docs.mongodb.com/manual/reference/mongo-shell/#command-helpers`) are not available for use, as they are not valid JavaScript functions.

Here is an example of a shell script that inserts three customers, and after each insert, unsets the `password` field. Note that you cannot issue the command `use <database>` to select the database, as you would inside the shell. As this is a script, you need to create a `Mongo` object instance, and then run the `getDB()` method to make the database connection:

```
insert_three.js ✖
conn = new Mongo();
db = conn.getDB("sweetscomplete");
db.customers.insertOne({"name":"Karyn Francis","address":"871 Rocky Autumn Mews","city":"Gassaway",
                        "state_province":"","postal_code":"RF21 26MI","country":"UK","phone":"385-836-7870",
                        "balance":"919.76","email":"karyn.francis@fastnet.com","password":"the9642He"});
db.customers.updateOne({"email":"karyn.francis@fastnet.com"},{$unset:{"password":1}});
db.customers.insertOne({"name":"Blanca Le","address":"179 Noble Pine Place","city":"Diagonal",
                        "state_province":"NS","postal_code":"B6R 2T3","country":"CA","phone":"185-787-5938",
                        "balance":"833.32","email":"blanca.le@telecom.com","password":"and6425said"});
db.customers.updateOne({"email":"blanca.le@telecom.com"},{$unset:{"password":1}});
db.customers.insertOne({"name":"Renee Decker","address":"42 Robbers Way","city":"Nome",
                        "state_province":"ACT","postal_code":"2900","country":"AU","phone":"660-333-4444",
                        "balance":"447.83","email":"renee.decker@westcom.net","password":"Stephens6135that"});
db.customers.updateOne({"email":"renee.decker@westcom.net"},{$unset:{"password":1}});
db.customers.insertOne({"name":"C.T. Russell","address":"123 Main Street","city":"New York",
                        "state_province":"NY","postal_code":"10001","country":"US","phone":"555-1212",
                        "balance":"0","email":"ctrussell@jw.org","password":"password"});
db.customers.updateOne({"email":"ctrussell@jw.org"},{$unset:{"password":1}});
```

We can then run the shell script from the command line, or from inside the shell using `load()`. Note that if you add the option `--shell`, after running the script, you are then taken to the mongo shell where you can verify the results:

```
fred@fred-linux:~$ mongo --shell Desktop/Repos/MongoDB_Quick_Start/Source/insert_three.js
MongoDB shell version v4.0.0
connecting to: mongodb://127.0.0.1:27017
MongoDB server version: 4.0.0
type "help" for help

sweetscomplete@fred-linux[up:1822]> db.customers.find({name:/Karyn|Blanca|Renee|C.T./},{name:1});
{ "_id" : ObjectId("5b3c49c67e8b700b9754d95b"), "name" : "Karyn Francis" }
{ "_id" : ObjectId("5b3c49c67e8b700b9754d95c"), "name" : "Blanca Le" }
{ "_id" : ObjectId("5b3c49c67e8b700b9754d95d"), "name" : "Renee Decker" }
{ "_id" : ObjectId("5b3c49c67e8b700b9754d95e"), "name" : "C.T. Russell" }
sweetscomplete@fred-linux[up:1822]> ▮
```

Most of the mongo command helpers have JavaScript equivalents. See the topic *Differences Between Interactive and Scripted mongo* (`https://docs.mongodb.com/manual/tutorial/write-scripts-for-the-mongo-shell/#differences-between-interactive-and-scripted-mongo`) in the MongoDB online manual for more information.

If you are already in the mongo shell, you can run an external JavaScript shell script using the `load(<filename.js>)` command. The script file must either be in the current directory, or you must specify the absolute path to the file, however, as `load()` has no search path.

Summary

In this chapter, you learned what the `mongo` shell is, and why you should use it. You also learned how to access the `mongo` shell, including several command-line options that allow you to run scripts and single commands. You then learned how to query the database from the command shell, with examples on how to define the *filter* and *projection*. After that, you learned how to add, edit, and delete using the command shell. Finally, you learned how to create and run a shell script.

In the next chapter, you'll learn about development using program language drivers.

4

Developing with Program Language Drivers

In `Chapter 3`, *Using the Mongo Shell*, you learned how to formulate basic CRUD operations using the JavaScript functions which the shell executed. In this chapter, you will learn how the same sort of operations can be performed using the PHP MongoDB driver. In addition, this chapter summarizes external PHP libraries and the integration of the Mongo PHP driver with various PHP frameworks.

The reason why PHP was chosen is because it is one of the most widely used web programming languages and is easy to understand, especially if you have a background in *C* language. Other popular languages such as *Java*, *JavaScript*, and *Python* are already well-documented on the MongoDB website (`https://docs.mongodb.com/ecosystem/drivers/`) and have plenty of examples, whereas this is not the case for PHP.

The version of PHP featured in this chapter is PHP 7.2. It's important to note that, even though we're going to be focusing on PHP, this chapter will be of critical interest to *all* developers.

The topics that we will learn about in this chapter are as follows:

- Overview of the MongoDB PHP driver
- Installing the MongoDB PHP extension
- Performing CRUD operations using PHPLIB
- Other libraries and framework integration

Overview of the MongoDB PHP driver

There are two primary PHP language drivers for MongoDB:

- The legacy mongo (http://php.net/manual/en/book.mongo.php) extension
- The recommended mongodb (http://php.net/manual/en/set.mongodb.php) extension

The original mongo extension was introduced in 2009. The latest version (1.6.16) was released in September 2017. It is now deprecated and its use is discouraged. The first stable version of the current extension was released in October 2016. At the time of writing this book, the most recent version was released 9 July 2018. For release information and direct access to the source code, go to http://pecl.php.net/package/mongodb.

MongoDB PHP architecture

The big difference between the old and new drivers is that the new driver is based upon libmongoc (https://github.com/mongodb/mongo-c-driver) and libbson (https://github.com/mongodb/mongo-c-driver/tree/master/src/libbson). Also, this extension provides support not only for PHP 5, but PHP 7 and even HHVM (https://hhvm.com/, a PHP code compatible abstraction layer used by Facebook). Finally, a library is provided which uses the mongodb extension, and provides all of the functionality which used to be included monolithically in the old extension. This means that MongoDB PHP developers are free to focus on adding value to PHP rather than having to do the low level work of connecting to MongoDB and extracting results.

The following diagram illustrates this separation of concerns:

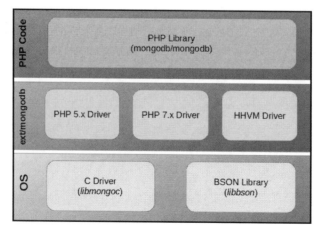

For more information, see the architectural overview of the MongoDB driver (`http://php.net/manual/en/mongodb.overview.php`) on `php.net`.

MongoDB PHP extension classes

The MongoDB PHP extension (which we will refer to simply as `ext/mongodb` for brevity) contains four main classes. Each class has its own PHP namespace. So, for example, if you wish to create an instance of the `MongoDB\Driver\Command` class, you would need to proceed as follows:

```php
<?php
 namespace Application;
 use MongoDB\Driver\Command;
 $command = new Command();
```

The main classes we will cover in this section are `MongoDB\Driver`, `MongoDB\BSON`, `MongoDB\Driver\Monitoring`, and `MongoDB\Driver\Exception`.

MongoDB\Driver classes

The `MongoDB\Driver` namespace includes 14 classes. Four of these classes allow for the manipulation of *read* and *write concerns*. Read concerns (`https://docs.mongodb.com/manual/reference/read-concern/#read-concern`) allow control over which replica set the data is drawn from. Write concerns (`https://docs.mongodb.com/manual/reference/write-concern/#write-concern`) control the level of acknowledgement between replicas. Read and write concerns are beyond the scope of this chapter, however. Please refer to `Chapter 6`, *Maintaining MongoDB Performance*, for more information.

Two of the classes, `Command` and `Query`, are *value objects*: objects which are used primarily as wrappers for various bits of functionality, and then thrown away (not stored or reused).

The class of the most interest is `Manager`, which does the following:

- Maintains the database connection
- Can communicate with a *local* server, replica set, or sharded cluster
- Does not immediately force a connection to a *mongos* instance
- Actual connections are *lazy-loaded* on demand

In this usage example, we are using `MongoDB\Driver\Manager` and `MongoDB\Driver\Query` to execute the following query:

```
//db.customers.find({country:/UK/,balance:{$lt:100}},
//{_id:0,name:1,email:1,country:1,postal_code:1});
$uri      = 'mongodb://localhost';
 $filter  = [
     'country' => 'UK',
     'balance' => ['$lt' => 100]
 ];
 $options = [
     'projection' => [
         '_id' => 0,
         'name' => 1,
         'email' => 1,
         'country' => 1,
         'postal_code' => 1
     ]
 ];
$manager = new MongoDB\Driver\Manager($uri);
$query   = new MongoDB\Driver\Query($filter, $options);
$cursor  = $manager->executeQuery('sweetscomplete.customers', $query);

foreach($cursor as $document) {
    vprintf(' %20s : %9s : %2s : %s' . PHP_EOL, (array) $document);
}
```

Here is the result:

```
  ● ● ●   Terminal
       Spencer Sanford :   PV9 74XN : UK : spencer.sanford@cablenet.net
          Jose Carter : HH34 64HU : UK : jose.carter@westcom.net
       Wilfredo Taylor :   MF6 8WM : UK : wilfredo.taylor@telecom.net
         Todd Lindsey :  FW38 8RB : UK : todd.lindsey@fastnet.net
                admin :     99999 : UK : admin@sweetscomplete.com


  - - - - - - - - - - - - - - -
  (program exited with code: 0)
  Press return to continue
```

MongoDB\BSON classes

BSON stands for Binary JSON (`http://bsonspec.org/`). The `MongoDB\BSON` namespace consists of the following:

- **6 functions**: 6 functions, which perform conversions between BSON, JSON, and PHP native data types

- **10 classes**: 10 classes, which represent BSON data types (for example, Binary, Timestamp, and so on)
- **13 interfaces**: 13 interfaces, which are used to formulate custom classes which meet a certain criteria

In addition, three classes called *DBPointer, Symbol,* and *Undefined* are included but deprecated, and thus they are not discussed here.

In this example, we are using the `MongoDB\BSON\Binary` to store a binary image of a flag, extracted from a `*.jpg` file:

```
use MongoDB\BSON\Binary;
use MongoDB\Driver\ {Manager, BulkWrite, Query};
```

Here is the logic which extracts a list of countries and the location flag graphics:

```
// Target URL:
$imagePattern =
'http://www.sciencekids.co.nz/images/pictures/flags96/%s.jpg';
$contents =
file_get_contents('http://www.sciencekids.co.nz/pictures/flags.html');
$pattern = '!img src="../images/pictures/flags96/(.+?).jpg" alt="Flag of
(.+?)" width="96!';
preg_match_all($pattern, $contents, $matches);
$flags = new ArrayIterator(array_combine($matches[1],$matches[2]));
```

Next, we set up the `MongoDB\Manager` and `BulkWrite` instances:

```
// setup MongoDB connection
$manager = new Manager('mongodb://localhost/mongodb_quickstart');
$bulk    = new BulkWrite(['ordered' => true]);

$startWith = 'C';
foreach ($flags as $img => $name) {
    if ($name[0] != $startWith) continue;
    echo 'Processing Flag for ' . $name . PHP_EOL;
    $imageSrc = sprintf($imagePattern, $img);
```

Notice how, inside the loop, we create `MongoDB\BSON\Binary` instances, which are then added to the bulk insert:

```
    $imageBson = new Binary(file_get_contents($imageSrc),
Binary::TYPE_GENERIC);
    // add to bulk insert
    $bulk->insert(['country' => $name, 'image' => $imageBson]);
}
```

We are now in a position to execute the bulk write, which is done off the `Manager` instance:

```php
// execute bulk write
 try {
     $result = $manager->executeBulkWrite('mongodb_quickstart.flags',
$bulk);
     echo 'Inserted ' . $result->getInsertedCount() . ' documents' .
PHP_EOL;
 } catch (MongoDB\Driver\Exception\BulkWriteException $e) {
     $result = $e;
 }

// view results
var_dump($result)
```

Here is the last part of the output when the preceding script is executed:

```
● ● ●   Terminal
Processing Flag for Cuba
Processing Flag for Cyprus
Processing Flag for Czech Republic
Inserted 16 documents
object(MongoDB\Driver\WriteResult)#4 (9) {
  ["nInserted"]=>
  int(16)
  ["nMatched"]=>
  int(0)
  ["nModified"]=>
  int(0)
  ["nRemoved"]=>
  int(0)
  ["nUpserted"]=>
  int(0)
  ["upsertedIds"]=>
  array(0) {
  }
  ["writeErrors"]=>
  array(0) {
  }
  ["writeConcernError"]=>
  NULL
  ["writeConcern"]=>
  object(MongoDB\Driver\WriteConcern)#5 (0) {
  }
}


------------------
(program exited with code: 0)
Press return to continue
```

The **image** field in each document now contains binary data which can then be extracted to re-display the image. If you open a mongo shell, you will note that the data is stored in *base64* (https://en.wikipedia.org/wiki/Base64) format.

MongoDB\Driver\ {Exception, Monitoring} classes

The ext/mongodb also provides Exception classes, which give information that is specific to MongoDB. Classes in the MongoDB\Driver\Exception namespace include AuthenticationException, CommandException, and WriteException, among others.

The MongoDB\Driver\Monitoring classes provide wrappers for the outcome of the various commands you might issue. Classes in this namespace include CommandFailedEvent, CommandStartedEvent, CommandSucceededEvent, CommandSubscriber, and Subscriber.

Installing the MongoDB PHP extension

In this section, we will cover the steps to install the MongoDB PHP extension on Windows and Linux/Mac. It is highly recommended for both Linux and macOS users to use *PECL* (http://pecl.php.net/) to install ext/mongodb. *PECL* stands for PHP Extension Community Library. It is a repository which contains PHP extensions that are written in C language, which must be compiled and enabled in the php.ini file. For a Windows installation, on the other hand, all you need to do is to install the appropriate *.dll file, and enable the extension in the php.ini file.

ext/mongodb installation using PECL

The **pecl** command is used for low level PHP engine packaging and distribution. This system is shared with **PEAR (PHP Extension and Application Repository)**, https://pear.php.net/. The latter contains libraries of functions written in PHP and is usually included in a standard PHP installation.

If, for some reason, the `pecl` command is not available on your system, install PEAR (`https://pear.php.net/manual/en/installation.introduction.php`), and also the PHP development library that is appropriate for your server (for example, `php-dev` for Debian/Ubuntu). It should be noted that when installing PHP extensions written in C, `pecl` will download the source and compile. This means that you also need to have a C compiler available (for example, `gcc`).

To compile `ext/mongodb` using PECL, enter the following command:

```
sudo pecl install mongodb
```

The results are shown here:

```
fred@fred-linux:~$ sudo pecl install mongodb
[sudo] password for fred:
WARNING: channel "pecl.php.net" has updated its protocols, use "pecl channel-update pecl.php.net"
 to update
downloading mongodb-1.5.0.tgz ...
Starting to download mongodb-1.5.0.tgz (1,054,840 bytes)
....done: 1,054,840 bytes
423 source files, building
running: phpize
Configuring for:
PHP Api Version:        20160303
Zend Module Api No:     20160303
Zend Extension Api No:  320160303
building in /tmp/pear/temp/pear-build-root1Uuvoi/mongodb-1.5.0
running: /tmp/pear/temp/mongodb/configure --with-php-config=/usr/local/bin/php-config
checking for grep that handles long lines and -e... /bin/grep
checking for egrep... /bin/grep -E
checking for a sed that does not truncate output... /bin/sed
checking for cc... cc
checking whether the C compiler works... yes
checking for C compiler default output file name... a.out
checking for suffix of executables...
checking whether we are cross compiling... no
checking for suffix of object files... o
checking whether we are using the GNU C compiler... yes
checking whether cc accepts -g... yes
checking for cc option to accept ISO C89... none needed
checking how to run the C preprocessor... cc -E
checking for icc... no
checking for suncc... no
checking whether cc understands -c and -o together... yes
checking for system library directory... lib
checking if compiler supports -R... no
```

When the compile process is finished, make a note of where the new extension binary has been placed:

```
Build process completed successfully
Installing '/usr/local/lib/php/extensions/no-debug-non-zts-20160303/mongodb.so'
install ok: channel://pecl.php.net/mongodb-1.5.0
configuration option "php_ini" is not set to php.ini location
You should add "extension=mongodb.so" to php.ini
fred@fred-linux:~$ █
```

Look in the php.ini file for your installation. If the directory indicated by the extension_dir directive does not match, you will first need to move the newly installed driver to that directory. If you are not sure where your php.ini file resides, use phpinfo() or php -i, as mentioned previously.

To activate the driver, add the following line to the php.ini file:

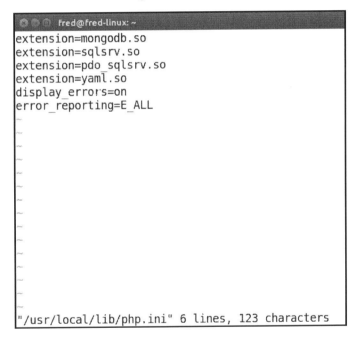

You can then confirm that the driver is operational by running `php -i` from the command line once more, or `phpinfo()` from a PHP script on a web server. The output from `php -i |grep mongo` is shown here:

```
fred@fred-linux: ~
fred@fred-linux:~$ php -i |grep mongo
mongodb
libmongoc bundled version => 1.11.0
libmongoc SSL => enabled
libmongoc SSL library => OpenSSL
libmongoc crypto => enabled
libmongoc crypto library => libcrypto
libmongoc crypto system profile => disabled
libmongoc SASL => disabled
libmongoc ICU => enabled
libmongoc compression => enabled
libmongoc compression snappy => disabled
libmongoc compression zlib => enabled
mongodb.debug => no value => no value
fred@fred-linux:~$
```

ext/mongodb installation on Windows

Installing the MongoDB PHP driver on Windows is actually quite simple:

1. Download the correct pre-compiled `*.dll` file from `http://pecl.php.net/package/mongodb`.
2. Add the following line to your installation's `php.ini` file:

```
extension=php_mongodb
```

The most difficult part is deciding *which* of the many pre-compiled `*.dll` files to use. From the `http://pecl.php.net/package/mongodb` page, choose the most appropriate MongoDB PHP Windows driver version (most likely the latest), and click on the link for *DLL*:

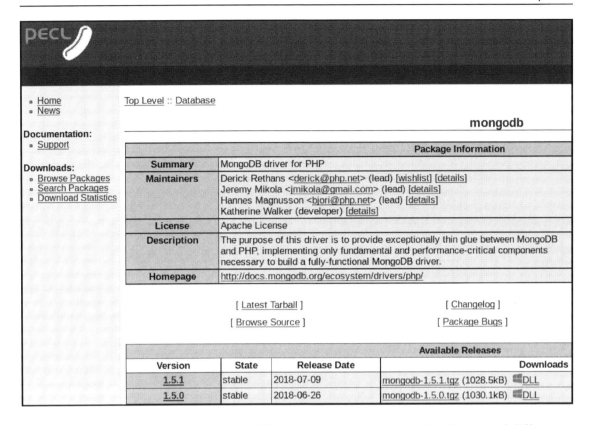

If you scroll down to the bottom of the DLL page, you are presented with several different versions of the `*.dll` file. In order to select the correct version, you need to find out some configuration information about your PHP/Windows installation:

- What version of PHP are you running (5.6, 7.0, 7.1, 7.2, and so on)?
- Is your PHP architecture 32 bit or 64 bit?
- Is *thread safety* (`https://stackoverflow.com/questions/7204758/php-thread-safe-and-non-thread-safe-for-windows#7204804`) enabled in the version of PHP that is installed?

You can find out the PHP version and architecture from either the command line or from a browser. If you plan to access MongoDB through a web server running on your Windows server, create a script as follows: `<?php phpinfo(); ?>`. If you plan to access MongoDB from the command line only, open a command prompt and enter `php -i |more`, which should look something like the illustration shown here:

Once you've determined the version of PHP and its architecture, here is a simple thread safety guideline which will assist you in choosing which version of the MongoDB Windows PHP Driver to use:

Running MongoDB from a Web Server?	Running PHP using FastCGI?	Version to Use
Yes	Yes	Non-Thread Safe
Yes	No	Thread Safe
No	N/A	Non-Thread Safe

Now, you can add the line mentioned previously to the `php.ini` file:

```
extension=php_mongodb
```

If you get an error when trying to use the newly installed MongoDB driver, try another driver.

The syntax `extension=xxx.dll/extension=xxx.so` has been deprecated. The new syntax is to omit `dll` or `so`. In the case of `ext/mongodb`, all you need to enter in the `php.ini` file is `extension=php_mongodb`.

To confirm that the driver is working, as mentioned previously, from a command prompt, simply run the following command:

```
php -i |more
```

If the MongoDB driver is not working, an error message will be displayed immediately at the top.

If you get this error ...
Warning: PHP Startup: Unable to load dynamic library 'php_mongodb.dll'
(tried: C:\path\to\php\ext\php_mongodb.dll (The specified module could not be found.) ...
... try different versions of the driver. If still not successful, try older versions of the driver.

Issues could arise on Windows depending on the compiler version that was used to compile the PHP binary. For example, XAMPP uses VC15 (PHP 7.2.8 on WIN32), but others (like WampServer) could be using VC11 or any other version of the Visual C compiler. It is therefore necessary to make sure that you download the corresponding DLL file.

Installing the PHP library for MongoDB (PHPLIB)

Once you have installed the low level extension `ext/mongodb`, the next step is to install the *PHP Library for MongoDB* (`http://php.net/manual/en/mongodb.tutorial.library.php`), which we will abbreviate as *PHPLIB*. Although it is not mandatory to install this library, directly using the classes provided by `ext/mongodb` would be tedious and require many lines of code. Why not use a library which is expressly designed to leverage `ext/mongodb` and provides a rich set of classes and functionality which would otherwise take you days or weeks to accomplish?

Although you could simply download the library directly from `https://github.com/mongodb/mongo-php-library`, it's probably best to install it using *Composer* (`https://getcomposer.org/`). There three distinct advantages to using Composer are as follows:

- Any dependencies this library has are automatically resolved
- Composer can also perform updates
- It includes an *auto-loader* which saves you having to use *include* or *require* statements in your PHP code

To obtain a copy of Composer, follow this link: `https://getcomposer.org/composer.phar`. To install *PHPLIB*, proceed as follows:

1. Open a terminal window (or command prompt)
2. Change to the directory containing your application source code
3. Use *Composer* to install PHPLIB:

```
php composer.phar require mongodb/mongodb
```

You will notice, from the following screenshot, that several things happen:

- A `vendor` folder is created
- *PHPLIB* is installed
- The Composer control file `composer.json` is created for future reference:

```
fred@fred-linux: ~/Desktop/Repos/MongoDB-Quick-Start-Guide-Doug/Source
fred@fred-linux:~/Desktop/Repos/MongoDB-Quick-Start-Guide-Doug/Source$
fred@fred-linux:~/Desktop/Repos/MongoDB-Quick-Start-Guide-Doug/Source$
php composer.phar require mongodb/mongodb
Using version ^1.4 for mongodb/mongodb
./composer.json has been created
Loading composer repositories with package information
Updating dependencies (including require-dev)
Package operations: 1 install, 0 updates, 0 removals
  - Installing mongodb/mongodb (1.4.0): Downloading (100%)
Writing lock file
Generating autoload files
fred@fred-linux:~/Desktop/Repos/MongoDB-Quick-Start-Guide-Doug/Source$
```

In order to start using *PHPLIB*, all you need to do is to add the following command at the beginning of your code:

```
require /path/to/source/vendor/autoload.php;
```

Performing CRUD operations using PHPLIB

Something of critical interest to developers is how to perform basic CRUD operations using `ext/mongodb`. You will note that *PHPLIB*, by design, is very closely modeled after the MongoDB JavaScript command set covered in `Chapter 3`, *Using the Mongo Shell*. The main difference is that instead of having arguments formulated as JSON expressions, when using *PHPLIB*, expressions use native PHP data types (for example, arrays, objects, and so on).

Core PHPLIB class instances needed for CRUD operations

It is important to note that all of the CRUD operations that we are going to discuss require that you create a `MongoDB\Collection` instance. This can be accomplished in several ways, including:

- `MongoDB\Client::selectCollection()`
- `MongoDB\Database::selectCollection()`
- `MongoDB\Collection::__construct()`

Of the three choices, we will focus on the first, since the `MongoDB\Client` consumes the database and thus provides more flexibility. To create a `MongoDB\Client` instance, proceed as follows:

1. First, define a `connection string URI` following this format:

   ```
   mongodb://[username:password@]host[:port][/[database][?options]]
   ```

2. Create a MongoDB\Client instance using the URI as an argument:

   ```
   $client = new MongoDB\Client(<connection_URI>);
   ```

For the purposes of this book, we define `Application\Client::getClient()`, which returns a `MongoDB\Client` instance:

```php
namespace Application;
 use Exception;
 use MongoDB\Client as MongoClient;
 class Client
 {
     protected $uri;
     protected $mongoClient;
     public function __construct($config)
     {
         $this->uri = $this->buildUri($config);
         $this->mongoClient = new MongoClient($this->uri);
     }
     public function getClient()
     {
         return $this->mongoClient;
     }

public function buildUri($config)
     {
// NOTE: not all code shown to conserve space: complete class available in
the repository
         $uri = 'mongodb://';
         if (!isset($config['host'])) {
             throw new Exception(self::ERROR_HOST);
         }
         $uri .= $config['host'];
         $uri .= (isset($config['database'])) ? '/' . $config['database'] :
'';
         return $uri;
     }
 }
```

Creating documents

In order to create new documents, you can use any of the following methods:

- `MongoDB\Collection::insertOne()`
- `MongoDB\Collection::insertMany()`
- `MongoDB\Collection::bulkWrite()`

Obviously, the last two are convenient when you want to insert multiple documents in one operation. The main downside to the last two methods, as defined in PHPLIB, is that you need to provide an array of documents. This takes up memory and might not be appropriate when a massive amount of data needs to be inserted.

In this example, however, the CSV file only contains 82 entries, and thus `insertMany()` is used:

```
// initialize env
require __DIR__ . '/vendor/autoload.php';
use Application\ {Client, Csv};

// set up mongodb client + collection
$params = ['host' => '127.0.0.1'];
$client = (new Client($params))->getClient();
$collection = $client->sweetscomplete->customers;

// empty out collection
$collection->drop();
$collection = $client->sweetscomplete->customers;

// set up CSV file processing
$csv = new Csv(__DIR__ . '/sweets_customers.csv');

// perform inserts
$insert = [];
foreach ($csv->getIteratorWithHeaders() as $data) {
    $data['balance'] = (float) $data['balance'];
    $data['password'] = password_hash($data['password'], PASSWORD_BCRYPT);
    $insert[] = $data;
}

try {
    $result = $collection->insertMany($insert);
    echo $result->getInsertedCount() . ' documents inserted' . PHP_EOL;
} catch (Exception $e) {
    echo $e->getMessage();
}
```

Here is the resulting output which confirms that 82 documents were inserted:

```
Terminal
82 documents inserted


------------------
(program exited with code: 0)
Press return to continue
```

We then run a *mongo* shell to confirm the results:

```
fred@fred-linux: ~/Desktop/Repos/MongoDB-Quick-Start-Guide-Doug
sweetscomplete@fred-linux[up:708003]> db.customers.find().count();
82
sweetscomplete@fred-linux[up:708003]> db.customers.find({},{name:1});
{ "_id" : ObjectId("5b47108b533b8406ac227792"), "name" : "name" }
{ "_id" : ObjectId("5b47108b533b8406ac227793"), "name" : "Conrad Perry" }
{ "_id" : ObjectId("5b47108b533b8406ac227794"), "name" : "Lonnie Knapp" }
{ "_id" : ObjectId("5b47108b533b8406ac227795"), "name" : "Darrel Roman" }
{ "_id" : ObjectId("5b47108b533b8406ac227796"), "name" : "Morgan Avila" }
{ "_id" : ObjectId("5b47108b533b8406ac227797"), "name" : "Lee Mccray" }
{ "_id" : ObjectId("5b47108b533b8406ac227798"), "name" : "Spencer Sanford" }
{ "_id" : ObjectId("5b47108b533b8406ac227799"), "name" : "Thomas Kirby" }
{ "_id" : ObjectId("5b47108b533b8406ac22779a"), "name" : "Brian Crawford" }
{ "_id" : ObjectId("5b47108b533b8406ac22779b"), "name" : "Armando Barlow" }
{ "_id" : ObjectId("5b47108b533b8406ac22779c"), "name" : "Jess Rocha" }
{ "_id" : ObjectId("5b47108b533b8406ac22779d"), "name" : "Felix Blevins" }
{ "_id" : ObjectId("5b47108b533b8406ac22779e"), "name" : "Jose Carter" }
{ "_id" : ObjectId("5b47108b533b8406ac22779f"), "name" : "Orlando Fulton" }
{ "_id" : ObjectId("5b47108b533b8406ac2277a0"), "name" : "Mitchell Roth" }
{ "_id" : ObjectId("5b47108b533b8406ac2277a1"), "name" : "Eduardo Wright" }
{ "_id" : ObjectId("5b47108b533b8406ac2277a2"), "name" : "Marc Ellis" }
{ "_id" : ObjectId("5b47108b533b8406ac2277a3"), "name" : "Joaquin Moses" }
{ "_id" : ObjectId("5b47108b533b8406ac2277a4"), "name" : "Morris Vargas" }
{ "_id" : ObjectId("5b47108b533b8406ac2277a5"), "name" : "Gene Cruz" }
Type "it" for more
sweetscomplete@fred-linux[up:708003]>
```

Reading documents

You will note that *PHPLIB* closely mirrors the JavaScript API. In order to read (query) the database, these two methods are the ones that are used the most:

- MongoDB\Collection::find()
- MongoDB\Collection::findOne()

In addition, *PHPLIB* includes methods to find and then replace, update, or delete:

- MongoDB\Collection::findOneAndDelete()
- MongoDB\Collection::findOneAndReplace()
- MongoDB\Collection::findOneAndUpdate()

In this example, we wish to reproduce this JavaScript command using *PHPLIB*:

```
db.customers.find(
    {country:/UK/,balance:{$lt:100}},
    {_id:0,name:1,email:1,phone:1,balance:1}
).sort({balance:1});
```

First, we initialize the environment:

```
require __DIR__ . '/vendor/autoload.php';
use MongoDB\BSON\Regex;
use Application\ {Client, Csv};
```

Next, we set up the client and collection:

```
$params = ['host' => '127.0.0.1'];
$client = (new Client($params))->getClient();
$collection = $client->sweetscomplete->customers;
```

We then define the *filter* and *options*. Note that, unlike its JavaScript equivalent, when using *PHPLIB*, the second argument is not the *projection*, but rather a set of options which includes keys for projection, sort, limit, and so on:

```
$filter = ['country' => new Regex('UK'),
           'balance' => ['$lt' => 100]];
$options = ['projection' =>
['name'=>1,'email'=>1,'phone'=>1,'balance'=>1],
           'sort'        => ['balance' => 1]];
```

Note the use of **MongoDB\BSON\Regex** to formulate a regular expression '/UK/'.

Finally, we execute the query and display the results:

```
try {
    $cursor = $collection->find($filter, $options);
    foreach ($cursor as $document) {
        printf(' %16s : %30s : %12s : %6.2f' . PHP_EOL,
            $document->name, $document->email, $document->phone,
$document->balance);
    }
} catch (Exception $e) {
    echo $e->getMessage();
}
```

Here is the output:

```
Terminal
 Spencer Sanford :    spencer.sanford@cablenet.net : 451-815-7386 :   -7.61
           admin :       admin@sweetscomplete.com : 000-000-000 :    0.00
 Wilfredo Taylor :    wilfredo.taylor@telecom.net : 126-579-1787 :   25.11
    Todd Lindsey :       todd.lindsey@fastnet.net : 565-309-4959 :   48.91
     Jose Carter :        jose.carter@westcom.net : 176-111-1052 :   56.22


------------------
(program exited with code: 0)
Press return to continue
```

You do not have to suppress the _id field when using *PHPLIB*. (the projection does not need to contain {_id:0}.)

Searching by ObjectId

In the legacy RDBMS world, developers are used to performing searches based on the *primary key*. In MongoDB, there is no concept of a primary key, as each document can be completely different from others, including having a completely different mix of fields. Accordingly, in order to keep the collection organized, MongoDB auto-generates an **ObjectId** instance. This is guaranteed to be unique among servers, replicas, and shards. It is created from the UNIX timestamp, a machine identifier, process ID, and a random value.

In order to perform a search based on this value, you can use the
`MongoDB\BSON\ObjectId` class. To demonstrate how this works, let's work off the search
we showed you previously. For illustration purposes, we just want to locate the document
for the fictitious customer *Spencer Sanford*. From the `mongo` shell, we issue the following
query:

```
db.customers.find({name:/Spencer/});
```

We then try to search directly on the _id field. However, there are no results. This is clearly
visible from the `mongo` shell:

```
fred@fred-linux: ~/Desktop/Repos/MongoDB-Quick-Start-Guide-Doug/Source/Chapter04
sweetscomplete@fred-linux[up:110]> db.customers.find({name:/Spencer/});
{ "_id" : ObjectId("5b47108b533b8406ac227798"), "name" : "Spencer Sanford", "address" : "620 Colon
ial Autumn Meadow", "city" : "Nooseneck", "state_province" : "", "postal_code" : "PV9 74XN", "coun
try" : "UK", "phone" : "451-815-7386", "balance" : -7.61, "email" : "spencer.sanford@cablenet.net"
, "password" : "$2y$10$E9bGbfoeCN9GBJ2asveMI.EO5Lbl7YwlB2Waw9r3pHj5KxWKCL7Fi" }
sweetscomplete@fred-linux[up:110]> db.customers.find({_id:"5b47108b533b8406ac227798"});
sweetscomplete@fred-linux[up:110]>
```

The solution is to formulate the search using a `MongoDB\BSON\ObjectId` instance. For this
purpose, we will take the preceding code but modify the *filter* to perform the search:

```
$filter = ['_id' => new MongoDB\BSON\ObjectId('5b47108b533b8406ac227798')];
 try {
     $document = $collection->findOne($filter);
     echo $document->name . PHP_EOL;
     var_dump($document->_id);
 } catch (Exception $e) {
     echo $e->getMessage();
 }
```

Here are the results:

```
Terminal
Spencer Sanford
object(MongoDB\BSON\ObjectId)#18 (1) {
  ["oid"]=>
  string(24) "5b47108b533b8406ac227798"
}


------------------
(program exited with code: 0)
Press return to continue
```

To perform the same query (search by `ObjectId`) from the `mongo` shell, here is how the preceding search would appear:
`db.customers.find(ObjectId("5b47108b533b8406ac227798"));`

Updating documents

As with queries, when performing updates, PHPLIB closely mirrors the JavaScript equivalent. Thus, the following methods are available:

- `MongoDB\Collection::replaceOne()`
- `MongoDB\Collection::updateOne()`
- `MongoDB\Collection::updateMany()`
- `MongoDB\Collection::findOneAndReplace()`
- `MongoDB\Collection::findOneAndUpdate()`

In this example, we will use the same filter as we did previously (the `ObjectID` for the customer `Spencer Sanford`) and update the balance:

```
// here is the JavaScript query we wish to emulate:
// db.customers.updateOne(
//      {_id:ObjectId("5b47108b533b8406ac227798")},
//      {$set:{balance:99.99}}
// );

$filter = ['_id' => new ObjectId('5b47108b533b8406ac227798')];
try {
    $document = $collection->findOne($filter);
    printf("Name: %s | Old Balance: %.2f\n", $document->name,
$document->balance);
    $data = ['$set' => ['balance' => 99.99]];
    $result = $collection->updateOne($filter, $data);
    printf("Matched %d document(s)\n", $result->getMatchedCount());
    printf("Modified %d document(s)\n", $result->getModifiedCount());
    $document = $collection->findOne($filter);
    printf("Name: %s | New Balance: %.2f\n", $document->name,
$document->balance);
} catch (Exception $e) {
    echo $e->getMessage();
}
```

Here is the output:

```
Terminal
Name: Spencer Sanford | Old Balance: -7.61
Matched 1 document(s)
Modified 1 document(s)
Name: Spencer Sanford | New Balance: 99.99


-------------------
(program exited with code: 0)
Press return to continue
```

Deleting documents

To delete documents from the collection using *PHPLIB*, we can use either of the following:

- MongoDB\Collection::deleteOne()
- MongoDB\Collection::deleteMany()

In this example, we first perform a find() to confirm the filter. After confirmation we issue a deleteMany() command to will remove all customers whose balance is less than or equal to zero, but whose name is not admin. Here is the JavaScript command we wish emulate:

```
db.customers.deleteMany({balance:{$lte:0},name:{$ne:"admin"}},{name:1});
```

The initial setup is exactly like the previous example (we create an Application\Client instance). The setup for the filter which emulates the preceding JavaScript command looks like this:

```
$filter = [
    'balance' => ['$lte' => 0],
    'name'    => ['$ne' => 'admin']
];
$options = ['projection' => ['name' => 1, 'balance' => 1]];
```

We then test to see if the *Delete* button has been pressed. If so, we execute deleteMany(). Otherwise, we execute find(), using the same filter and projection:

```
$cursor  = [];
$message = '';
try {
    if (isset($_POST['delete'])) {
```

```
          $result = $collection->deleteMany($filter);
          $message = 'Deleted ' . $result->getDeletedCount() . '
document(s)';
    } else {
          $cursor = $collection->find($filter,$options);
    }
} catch (Exception $e) {
    echo $e->getMessage();
} ?>
```

Finally, we present a simple HTML form:

```
<html>
 <body>
 <b>Delete These Customers?</b>
 <pre>
 <?php foreach ($cursor as $document)
      printf('%20s : %6.2f' . PHP_EOL, $document->name, $document->balance)
?>
 </pre>
 </table>
 <form method="post">
 <input name="delete" value="Delete" type="submit" />
 <input name="cancel" value="Cancel" type="submit" />
 </form>
 <b style="color:red;"><?= $message ?></b>
 </body>
 </html>
Here is the initial HTML screen:
```

Delete These Customers?

```
           name :   0.00
Spencer Sanford :  -7.61
Samuel Harding : -11.56
  Lauri Grimes : -37.95
         Obama :   0.00
  C.T. Russell :   0.00
```

[Delete] [Cancel]

And here is the result after pressing the **Delete** button:

Delete These Customers?

Delete   Cancel

Deleted 6 document(s)

> Before performing any delete operation, it is highly recommended that you first test the filter using `find()`!

Other libraries and framework integration

There are a number of PHP packages which are based upon the MongoDB Driver for PHP (which is to say `ext/mongodb` and *PHPLIB)*. These packages can be installed using Composer, and are listed on `packagist.org`. The following table summarizes these packages. If a package is not specifically designed for any particular framework, it is marked in the table as *standalone*. The packages are listed in order of the number of downloads, as recorded by the Packagist website. Packages with less than 200,000 downloads are not included:

Package	*Works With ...*	*Notes*
`jenssegers/mongodb`	Laravel	Mini-framework for building a library of commonly used model classes. Supports the *Eloquent* set of models with a query builder.
`doctrine/mongodb` `doctrine/mongodb-odm`	Doctrine	Provides *Object Document Mapping* capabilities to MongoDB via the `Doctrine Project`.
`phpfastcache/phpfastcache`	PhpFastCache	MongoDB driver for this caching library.
`friendsofsymfony/ elastica-bundle`	Symfony	For Symfony applications using Elastica (search engine), this provides support for MongoDB.
`doctrine/ mongodb-odm-bundle`	Symfony	Database handling for Symfony applications is handled by Doctrine. This package provides MongoDB support for the Doctrine/Symfony integration.
`sonata-project/cache`	N/A	Provides caching to your application based on MongoDB.
`alcaeus/mongo-php-adapter`	N/A	Provides a bridge between the original `ext/mongo` and the current `ext/mongodb` extensions.
`analog/analog`	N/A	Generic logging class, which includes a driver for MongoDB.
`yiisoft/yii2-mongodb`	Yii	Adds MongoDB support to the Yii framework.
`dg/adminer-custom`	Adminer	Adds MongoDB support to this database managment tool.

Summary

In this chapter, you learned how to access MongoDB from PHP. You learned that there are two extensions, `ext/mongo`, which has been deprecated, and `ext/mongodb`. The latter extension actually consists of three layers: low level libraries supplied by the OS, drivers for PHP 5, PHP 7, and HVVM, and a high level library called *PHPLIB*. You then learned that installation on Windows involves choosing the right `*.dll` file based on your PHP installation, whereas for Linux and Mac it is recommended to perform the installation using PECL.

You learned how to perform Create, Read, Update, and Delete operations using *PHPLIB*. You also learned that you cannot directly search the auto-generated object ID, but rather need to create an `ObjectId` instance first, and then use that in the search. Finally, you learned that there are many PHP libraries for MongoDB which are available on the Packagist website.

In the next chapter, you will learn advanced query techniques as well as *cursor* treatments for using MongoDB's *aggregation* features.

5
Building Complex Queries Using Aggregation

The focus of this chapter will be on a feature that's unique to MongoDB called the Aggregation Framework (`https://www.mongodb.com/presentations/aggregation-framework-0?jmp=docs_ga=2.166048830.1278448947.1531711178-137143613.1528093145`), which is vital when forming complex queries. This feature allows database developers, or DBAs, to return subsets of data that are grouped, sorted, and filtered. We will start our discussion by forming a simple aggregation using *single-purpose methods* (`https://docs.mongodb.com/manual/aggregation/#single-purpose-aggregation-operations`). After that, we will get into the more complex topics of forming an *aggregation pipeline* (`https://docs.mongodb.com/manual/aggregation/#aggregation-pipeline`) and making use of the *map-reduce* (`https://docs.mongodb.com/manual/aggregation/#map-reduce`) function. We will also show you how to perform operations on a complex document that contains embedded objects.

The topics that are going to be covered in this chapter are as follows:

- An overview of aggregation
- Using single-purpose aggregation
- Using the aggregation pipeline
- Using map-reduce
- Using the MongoDB Compass aggregation pipeline builder

An overview of aggregation

Before diving into the specifics, it's important to lay some groundwork. The first question which comes to mind is, *What is aggregation*? That question would be logically followed by, *Why use it?*

What is aggregation?

The main purpose of aggregation operations is to refine query results by grouping together field values from multiple documents, and then performing one or more transformations. Aggregation in MongoDB can be as simple as presenting the results of a query into a set of one or more fields, or as complex as performing a multistage query, breaking the output into *buckets*, and performing operations on each result set. A more advanced usage would be to manipulate complex fields within a document. For example, if a document contains an array as one of its fields, an aggregation pipeline could be used to filter the output from this array.

The closest SQL equivalent to MongoDB aggregation would be the LIMIT, GROUP BY, and ORDER BY clauses, and the SQL functions AVG(), SUM(), COUNT(), and so on. Even JOIN and subselects could be construed as a form of aggregation in SQL. MongoDB aggregation can accomplish all of these operations and much more!

Why use aggregation?

A practical use for single-purpose aggregation is to present results in a certain order (via sorting), and limiting the number of results which appear at the end of a query. A more complex form of aggregation, the aggregation pipeline, might be used to:

- Manipulate documents, which include embedded objects or arrays
- Optimize results when operating on a *sharded cluster* (https://docs.mongodb.com/manual/sharding/#sharded-cluster)

In the former case, single-purpose aggregation is not useful if you want to sort the values in an array, which is embedded in a document. As for the latter case, a *sharded cluster* is where you have a subset of the database distributed across a set of servers which are networked together. Aggregation pipelines and map-reduce functions can operate in parallel across the sharded cluster, which greatly enhances overall performance. The mongos (much like routers for the database) can target the query for a specific shard or set of shards, which offers much better efficiency than simply broadcasting the query to all networked database servers.

The MongoDB documentation recommends using aggregation pipelines over map-reduce functions as the pipeline approach uses native MongoDB classes and methods.

Using single-purpose aggregation

Single-purpose aggregation operators are available so that you can operate on a *collection* or a *cursor*. The following table summarizes the operators which can operate on a collection:

db.collection.count()	Wraps the $count aggregation operator to produce the number of documents in a collection.
db.collection.distinct()	Wrapper for the distinct command (https://docs.mongodb.com/manual/reference/command/distinct/#distinct). Produces distinct values for document fields across a collection.

The following table summarizes single-purpose aggregation operations which can be performed on a cursor (such as the iteration returned after executing db.collection.find()):

cursor.count()	Equivalent to db.collection.count() (see prior table)
cursor.limit()	Limits the number of documents in the final result
cursor.sort()	Returns the results in the order specified

> MongoDB provides the single-purpose cursor aggregation methods min() and max(), however these require an index on the field, which is used to determine the minimum or maximum. It might be easier to use db.collection.find() and the $gt and/or $lt operators instead.

The following example produces a count of customers from the UK:

```
fred@fred-linux: ~/Desktop/Repos/MongoDB-Quick-Start-Guide-Doug
sweetscomplete@fred-linux[up:344837]> db.customers.find({country:/UK/}).count();
22
sweetscomplete@fred-linux[up:344837]>
```

While the following example produces a list of distinct countries from the customers collection:

```
fred@fred-linux: ~/Desktop/Repos/MongoDB-Quick-Start-Guide-Doug
sweetscomplete@fred-linux[up:344837]> db.customers.distinct("country");
[ "CA", "US", "AU", "UK" ]
sweetscomplete@fred-linux[up:344837]>
```

It is important to note that, while single-purpose aggregation operators are easy to use, they do not have the sophistication to handle complex documents, nor do they offer any flexibility.

Using the aggregation pipeline

The MongoDB *aggregation pipeline framework* consists of the `aggregate()` collection method, and a sequence of operations referred to as *stages* (`https://docs.mongodb.com/manual/reference/operator/aggregation-pipeline/#aggregation-pipeline-stages`). This sequence is referred to as a *pipeline*.

For illustration, let's assume that there's a collection called `purchases`, where each purchase has an amount of information as well as embedded `customer` and `product` objects:

```
{
    "_id" : ObjectId("5b500ad8533b844173064593"),

    "customer" : {
        "_id" : ObjectId("5b482b45533b843e7b6f70c5"),
        "name" : "Darrel Roman",
        "state_province" : "NT",
        "country" : "AU",
        "balance" : 357.51
    },

    "product" : {
        "_id" : ObjectId("5b4c232accf2ea73a85ed2b4"),
        "sku" : "C3000",
        "title" : "Chocolate Angelfood Cupcakes",
        "price" : 0.3
    },

    "date" : "2017-12-30",
    "quantity" : 71,
    "amount" : 21.3
}
```

We wish to generate a report on the total sales for each customer from Australia. A simple `db.collection.find()` command will not suffice as it is incapable of grouping the customers. The problem is further compounded by the fact that country information is embedded in the `customer` object within each purchase. In order to generate this report, we will first need to address stages.

> Be sure to bookmark this page when formulating commands using an aggregation pipeline:
> `https://docs.mongodb.com/manual/meta/aggregation-quick-reference/#aggregation-pipeline-quick-reference`.

Aggregation pipeline stages

The aggregation pipeline stages are represented by *stage operators*. In the following illustration, we formulate a command which has two stages. The first stage performs a match (see the discussion of the `$match` operator that follows), followed by a grouping stage (see `$group`). You can have as many or as few stages as desired. Each stage produces results which are put back into the *pipeline*, and subsequently processed by the next stage:

```
db.purchases.aggregate( [

    { $match : { "customer.country":"/AU/" } },                   MATCH STAGE

    { $group : { _id  : "$customer.name",
              total : { $sum : "$amount" } } }                    GROUP STAGE

] );
```

The discussion in this section summarizes key stage operators, which can be used in conjunction with the `db.collection.aggregate()` command. The examples shown here assume that there's a collection of `purchases`, like the ones we described previously. Please note that we only cover certain key stages here. For a complete reference, see in the documentation *Aggregation Pipeline Stages* (`https://docs.mongodb.com/manual/reference/operator/aggregation-pipeline/#aggregation-pipeline-stages`).

> In the simple query shown in the preceding graphic, please note the difference between `customer.country` and `$customer.name`. The `customer` is the embedded object, and `country` and `name` are properties of this object. Both references need to be in quotes so that the parser knows that we are referring to a compound property name. If you place a field in quotes, but precede it with a dollar sign (for example, `$customer.name`), the parser will return the *value* of the field.

$bucket

This stage operator allows you to break up the output into a set of distinct arrays called *buckets*. The criteria used to separate documents into buckets is determined by the field identified with the groupBy parameter. This parameter matches the document field against the limits specified by the boundaries parameter. The values in boundaries can be either numeric or strings.

In the following example, we break up the query into buckets based on name. The boundary ["A", "G", "M", "S", "Y"] means that multiple buckets will be formed based on customer names A-F, G-L, M-R, and S-X. The Y and Z will fall into the "default." We then use the $project stage to produce a sum of the amounts for this group of customers:

```
 ●●●    fred@fred-linux: ~/Desktop/Repos/MongoDB-Quick-Start-Guide-Doug
sweetscomplete@fred-linux[up:965]> db.purchases.aggregate( [
... {
...       $bucket: {
...         groupBy: "$customer.name",
...         boundaries: [ "A", "G", "M", "S", "Y" ],
...         default: "Y-Z",
...         output: {
...           "count": { $sum: 1 },
...           "names" : { $push: "$customer.name" },
...           "amounts" : { $push: "$amount"}
...         }
...       }
... },
... {
...       $project: {
...           _id : "$_id",
...           count : "$count",
...           amounts : { $sum: "$amounts" }
...       }
... }
... ] );
{ "_id" : "A", "count" : 263, "amounts" : 44894.1 }
{ "_id" : "G", "count" : 325, "amounts" : 51267.2 }
{ "_id" : "M", "count" : 173, "amounts" : 25485.5 }
{ "_id" : "S", "count" : 51, "amounts" : 6113.2 }
{ "_id" : "Y-Z", "count" : 18, "amounts" : 2726.5 }
sweetscomplete@fred-linux[up:965]>
```

$group

The `$group` stage operator allows you to aggregate on a specific field. You can then apply *accumulator operators* (`https://docs.mongodb.com/manual/reference/operator/aggregation/group/#accumulator-operator`) to the result in order to produce sums, averages, and so on. Here is an example query which produces totals by customer name, including the average quantity and the total number of purchases. Note that the _id field represents the grouping criteria. The other field names (`total`, `avgQty`, and `count`) are arbitrarily chosen:

```
fred@fred-linux: ~/Desktop/Repos/MongoDB-Quick-Start-Guide-Doug
sweetscomplete@fred-linux[up:344837]> db.purchases.aggregate( [
...     { $group: {
...         _id: "$customer.name",
...         total: { $sum: "$amount" },
...         avgQty: { $avg: "$quantity" },
...         count: { $sum: 1 }
...       }
...     },
... ] );
{ "_id" : "admin", "total" : 963.1, "avgQty" : 50.833333333333336, "count" : 6 }
{ "_id" : "Renee Decker", "total" : 2254.2, "avgQty" : 43.666666666666664, "count" : 15 }
{ "_id" : "Louella Allen", "total" : 1964.9, "avgQty" : 51.07692307692308, "count" : 13 }
{ "_id" : "Elba Mccall", "total" : 2145.7, "avgQty" : 48.06666666666667, "count" : 15 }
{ "_id" : "Socorro Jimenez", "total" : 133, "avgQty" : 95, "count" : 1 }
{ "_id" : "Fannie Moore", "total" : 3210.4, "avgQty" : 44.5, "count" : 16 }
{ "_id" : "Josefina Hampton", "total" : 2046.8, "avgQty" : 37.5625, "count" : 16 }
{ "_id" : "Lucille Bradford", "total" : 95, "avgQty" : 95, "count" : 1 }
{ "_id" : "Geneva Case", "total" : 551.9, "avgQty" : 67.33333333333333, "count" : 3 }
{ "_id" : "Jaime Noel", "total" : 2692.4, "avgQty" : 57.166666666666664, "count" : 18 }
{ "_id" : "Isabel Rodriguez", "total" : 2953.9, "avgQty" : 59.642857142857146, "count" : 14 }
{ "_id" : "Jami Ruiz", "total" : 2393.8, "avgQty" : 48.23529411764706, "count" : 17 }
{ "_id" : "Aileen Duncan", "total" : 1098.3, "avgQty" : 46.142857142857146, "count" : 7 }
{ "_id" : "Denis Snider", "total" : 140, "avgQty" : 43.666666666666664, "count" : 3 }
{ "_id" : "Todd Lindsey", "total" : 466.5, "avgQty" : 49.333333333333336, "count" : 6 }
{ "_id" : "Garrett Campos", "total" : 3432.1, "avgQty" : 51.294117647058826, "count" : 17 }
{ "_id" : "Hans Page", "total" : 919.9, "avgQty" : 45.77777777777778, "count" : 9 }
{ "_id" : "Ramiro Bentley", "total" : 1475.2, "avgQty" : 56.083333333333336, "count" : 12 }
{ "_id" : "Jesus Bright", "total" : 1351.9, "avgQty" : 43.81818181818182, "count" : 11 }
{ "_id" : "Cecelia Case", "total" : 3690.7, "avgQty" : 57.88235294117647, "count" : 17 }
Type "it" for more
sweetscomplete@fred-linux[up:344837]>
```

$lookup

Similar to an SQL LEFT OUTER JOIN, $lookup allows you to incorporate documents from another collection. The following example shows a purchases document with an embedded joined customers document. In this example, there are three stages: $lookup, $limit, and $project. Note that in the $project stage we suppress the already embedded customer field as it only contains a partial subset of customer information:

```
fred@fred-linux: ~/Desktop/Repos/MongoDB-Quick-Start-Guide-Doug
sweetscomplete@fred-linux[up:344837]> db.purchases.aggregate([
...     { $lookup: {
...             from: "customers",
...             localField: "customer.name",
...             foreignField: "name",
...             as: "purch_plus_cust" }
...     },
...     { $limit: 1 },
...     { $project: { _id: 0, customer: 0, "purch_plus_cust.password": 0 } }
... ]).pretty();
{
        "product" : {
                "_id" : ObjectId("5b4c232accf2ea73a85ed2c7"),
                "sku" : "C22000",
                "title" : "Chocolate Toaster Tarts",
                "price" : 2.2
        },
        "date" : "2017-09-20",
        "quantity" : 15,
        "amount" : 33,
        "purch_plus_cust" : [
                {
                        "_id" : ObjectId("5b482b45533b843e7b6f70c3"),
                        "name" : "Conrad Perry",
                        "address" : "79 Amber Branch Falls",
                        "city" : "Birdseye",
                        "state_province" : "QC",
                        "postal_code" : "G0U 0M5",
                        "country" : "CA",
                        "phone" : "484-181-9811",
                        "balance" : 745.32,
                        "email" : "conrad.perry@fastmedia.com"
                }
        ]
}
sweetscomplete@fred-linux[up:344837]>
```

$match

This stage operator applies a filter to the final results, much like `db.collection.find()`. In the example shown here, we group by the product title and produce a sum of purchases for each title in order to match `chocolate` purchases in the *UK*:

```
fred@fred-linux: ~/Desktop/Repos/MongoDB-Quick-Start-Guide-Doug
sweetscomplete@fred-linux[up:344837]> db.purchases.aggregate( [
...      { $match: {
...              "customer.country":/UK/,
...              "product.title":/chocolate/i
...          }
...      },
...      { $group:   {
...              _id:"$product.title",
...              "total": {$sum:"$amount"}
...          }
...      }
... ] );
{ "_id" : "Chocolate Angelfood Cupcakes", "total" : 30.6 }
{ "_id" : "Mint Chocolate Milk Shake", "total" : 915.9 }
{ "_id" : "Chocolate Toaster Tarts", "total" : 286 }
{ "_id" : "Chocolate Fondue", "total" : 512 }
{ "_id" : "Chocolate Layer Cake", "total" : 695.4 }
{ "_id" : "Chocolate Mousse", "total" : 195 }
{ "_id" : "Chocolate Eclair", "total" : 562.8 }
{ "_id" : "Chocolate Soufflé", "total" : 561 }
{ "_id" : "Chocolate Chip Cookies", "total" : 160 }
sweetscomplete@fred-linux[up:344837]>
```

In addition, there are operators that produce results similar to the single-purpose aggregation operators, including `$count`, `$limit`, `$project`, and `$sort`. It is also worth mentioning that the `$unwind` stage operator can be used to *flatten* embedded arrays in order to provide easier access in subsequent stages.

Formulate your query to use `$match` as the first stage in order to optimize MongoDB indexes.

Aggregation pipeline expression operators

The following table summarizes the key aggregation pipeline operators (`https://docs.mongodb.com/manual/meta/aggregation-quick-reference/#operator-expressions`) that are currently available:

Arithmetic	This set currently consists of 15 basic operators, which let you perform arithmetic operations including `$add`, `$subtract`, `$multiply`, and so on.
Array	These operators are needed when a document contains an array property. Notable operators in this set include: • `$in`: Used to determine if a value is in an array or not • `$size`: Gives you the number of elements in the array • `$slice`: Returns a subset of the array
Boolean	Used to formulate complex conditions. These include `$and`, `$or`, and `$not`.
Comparison	Standard comparison operators between values including `$cmp` (compare), `$eq` (equal), `$ne` (not equal), `$gt` (greater than), `$gte` (greater than or equal), `$lt` (less than), and `$lte` (less than or equal).
Conditional	Used to formulate conditions. This set includes `$cond` (ternary if/then/else), `$ifNull` (first non-null expression), and `$switch` (standard C-like switch/case).
Date	This set currently consists of 18 date operators which include: • Converting between a date string and a BSON date object (for example, `$dateFromString`, `$dateToString`) • Day, week, and month (for example, `$dayOfMonth`, `$isoDayOfWeek`) • Hour, minute, and second (for example, `$hour`, `$minute`) Newly added in version 4.0 is `$toDate`, which converts a given value into a BSON date. It should also be noted that `$add` and `$subtract` can also handle date arithmetic.
Object	This set includes `$mergeObjects` and `$objectToArray`; both are self-explanatory.
String	These 18 operators perform string manipulation, and include `$concat` (concatinating strings), `$substr` (substring), and `$trim` (removing white space from beginnings and ends), among others.
Type	This group of 10 operators is used to perform data type conversion, and includes `$convert` (generic anything-to-anything coversion), `$toInt` (convert to integer), `$toString` (convert to string), and `$toObjectId` (converts a value to a BSON `ObjectId` object).

Aggregation pipeline accumulators

In addition to expression operators, there are a number of operators referred to as *accumulators* (https://docs.mongodb.com/manual/meta/aggregation-quick-reference/#accumulators-group), which are used in conjunction with $group, $project, and $addFields. This form of operator spans all the documents in the pipeline and produces an aggregate result.

$group stage accumulators

Accumulators, which can be used with the $group stage, include $avg (average), $sum (sum), $first, $last, $min (minimum), and $max (maximum). There are two which are used for *standard deviation*: $stdDevPop (population) and $stdDevSamp (sample). The $push operator produces an array of expression values for each group.

$project and $addFields stage accumulators

Accumulators available for use in $project and $addFields are the same operators that were mentioned in the previous section. Only $avg, $sum, $min, $max, $stdDevPop, and $stdDevSamp can be used with this stage, however. The example shown in the previous section demonstrated $sum, $min, and $push in the $project stage.

Aggregation pipeline expression operator examples

In this first example, we are going to generate a query to satisfy a management request for a report on buying patterns based on the day of the week. We are using the $bucket stage operator to produce seven arrays of purchases representing each day of the week. We will then group by $dayOfWeek, which in turn uses $toDate to produce a BSON Date instance. The $push will be used to copy the arrays out into the pipeline. We will then use the $project stage to produce the output, which consists of the day's number, the day's abbreviation, and the sum. In order to get the actual three-letter day abbreviation, we use the $arrayElemAt operator against the array days.

Note the use of $subtract to adjust the DOW to accommodate the 0-based array days. The $sum accumulator (discussed in the following example) provides a sum:

```
fred@fred-linux: ~/Desktop/Repos/MongoDB-Quick-Start-Guide-Doug
sweetscomplete@fred-linux[up:214862]>
days = ["Sun","Mon","Tue","Wed","Thu","Fri","Sat"];
[ "Sun", "Mon", "Tue", "Wed", "Thu", "Fri", "Sat" ]
sweetscomplete@fred-linux[up:214862]> db.purchases.aggregate( [
... {
...        $bucket: {
...           groupBy: { $dayOfWeek: { $toDate: "$date" } },
...           boundaries: [ 1,2,3,4,5,6,7,8 ],
...           default: "other",
...           output: {
...             "dow" : { $push: { $dayOfWeek: { $toDate: "$date" } } },
...             "amounts" : { $push: "$amount"}
...           }
...        }
... },
... {
...        $project: {
...           dow : { $min: "$dow" },
...           day : { $arrayElemAt: [days, { $subtract: [{ $min:"$dow" }, 1] }]},
...           amounts : { $sum: "$amounts" }
...        }
... }
... ] );
{ "_id" : 1, "dow" : 1, "day" : "Sun", "amounts" : 19364.5 }
{ "_id" : 2, "dow" : 2, "day" : "Mon", "amounts" : 14852.3 }
{ "_id" : 3, "dow" : 3, "day" : "Tue", "amounts" : 19859.5 }
{ "_id" : 4, "dow" : 4, "day" : "Wed", "amounts" : 21470.7 }
{ "_id" : 5, "dow" : 5, "day" : "Thu", "amounts" : 21182.7 }
{ "_id" : 6, "dow" : 6, "day" : "Fri", "amounts" : 16172.4 }
{ "_id" : 7, "dow" : 7, "day" : "Sat", "amounts" : 17584.4 }
sweetscomplete@fred-linux[up:214862]>
```

In the following example, we will start with a simple query which produces average purchases by quantity with *buckets* 0 – 9, 10 – 49, and 50 – 99 for customers in Australia. Note that the default *other* is included in the final tally:

```
fred@fred-linux: ~/Desktop/Repos/MongoDB-Quick-Start-Guide-Doug
sweetscomplete@fred-linux[up:214862]> db.purchases.aggregate( [
... { $match: { "customer.country": /AU/ } },
... {
...       $bucket: {
...         groupBy: "$quantity",
...         boundaries: [ 0,10,50,100 ],
...         default: "other",
...         output: {
...           "qty" : { $push: "$quantity" }
...         }
...       }
...    },
...    { $project: { qty : { $avg: "$qty" } } }
...    ] );
{ "_id" : 0, "qty" : 4.608695652173913 }
{ "_id" : 10, "qty" : 28.610526315789475 }
{ "_id" : 50, "qty" : 74.90677966101696 }
{ "_id" : "other", "qty" : 100 }
sweetscomplete@fred-linux[up:214862]>
```

In the revised version, we use `$cond` in the `$project` stage to formulate a condition using comparison operators. Note the use of the special operator `$$REMOVE` which, in this example, is used to remove *other*:

```
fred@fred-linux: ~/Desktop/Repos/MongoDB-Quick-Start-Guide-Doug
sweetscomplete@fred-linux[up:214862]> db.purchases.aggregate( [
... { $match: { "customer.country": /AU/ } },
... {
...       $bucket: {
...         groupBy: "$quantity",
...         boundaries: [ 0,10,50,100 ],
...         default: "other",
...         output: {
...           "qty" : { $push: "$quantity" }
...         }
...       }
...    },
...    {
...       $project: {
...           _id : { $cond: {if: { $eq: ["other", "$_id"] },
...                   then: "$$REMOVE",
...                   else: "$_id" }},
...           qty : { $cond: {if: { $eq: ["other", "$_id"] },
...                   then: "$$REMOVE",
...                   else: { $avg: "$qty" }}}
...       }
...    }
...    ] );
{ "_id" : 0, "qty" : 4.608695652173913 }
{ "_id" : 10, "qty" : 28.610526315789475 }
{ "_id" : 50, "qty" : 74.90677966101696 }
{  }
sweetscomplete@fred-linux[up:214862]>
```

There is an excellent presentation on aggregation pipeline optimization here: `https://docs.mongodb.com/manual/core/aggregation-pipeline-optimization/#aggregation-pipeline-optimization`.

Using map-reduce

The `db.collection.mapReduce()` method delivers similar results to that of the aggregation pipeline. The main difference is that rather than performing operations in *stages*, map-reduce uses JavaScript functions to produce results. This gives you access to the full programming power that's available in JavaScript. Because it operates outside of the aggregation framework, however, performance is generally worse. If there is a high degree of complexity in your query, it might be worth considering using this feature. Otherwise, the MongoDB documentation recommends using the aggregation pipeline framework.

To demonstrate map-reduce functionality, we will use the same `purchases` collection that we described previously. Here is the general structure of a `mapReduce()` command:

```
db.purchases.mapReduce(

    function() {
        if (this.customer.country == "US") {
            emit( this.customer.state_province, this.amount );     MAP
        }
    },

    function(key,values) {
        return Array.sum(values);                                  REDUCE
    },

    {
        query: { /* optional */ }                                  QUERY/
        out:   "totals_by_us_state_province"                       OUTPUT
    }

);
```

When we run this method, we get operational metadata. Unlike the `aggregate()` method, the output is placed into a separate collection named by the *out* directive. Note that we are performing filtering in the *map* segment. This could just as easily have been performed in the `query` segment, however. The command and its output are shown here:

```
● ● ●   fred@fred-linux: ~/Desktop/Repos/MongoDB-Quick-Start-Guide-Doug
sweetscomplete@fred-linux[up:214862]> db.purchases.mapReduce(
...        function() {
...             if (this.customer.country == "US") {
...                 emit( this.customer.state_province, this.amount );
...             }
...        },
...        function(key,values) { return Array.sum(values); },
...        {
...             out:    "totals_by_us_state_province"
...        }
... );
{
        "result" : "totals_by_us_state_province",
        "timeMillis" : 1616,
        "counts" : {
                "input" : 830,
                "emit" : 219,
                "reduce" : 16,
                "output" : 17
        },
        "ok" : 1
}
sweetscomplete@fred-linux[up:214862]>
```

We can then issue `find()` to view the output:

```
● ● ●   fred@fred-linux: ~/Desktop/Repos/MongoDB-Quick-Start-Guide-Doug
sweetscomplete@fred-linux[up:214862]> db.totals_by_us_state_province.find();
{ "_id" : "AK", "value" : 4849.4 }
{ "_id" : "AR", "value" : 3210.4 }
{ "_id" : "DE", "value" : 158.1 }
{ "_id" : "IN", "value" : 297 }
{ "_id" : "MA", "value" : 213.6 }
{ "_id" : "MT", "value" : 4740 }
{ "_id" : "ND", "value" : 988.6 }
{ "_id" : "NH", "value" : 2046.8000000000002 }
{ "_id" : "NM", "value" : 1351.9 }
{ "_id" : "OK", "value" : 1098.3 }
{ "_id" : "OR", "value" : 2353.8999999999996 }
{ "_id" : "RI", "value" : 956.9000000000001 }
{ "_id" : "SC", "value" : 4819.8 }
{ "_id" : "SD", "value" : 1475.2 }
{ "_id" : "TN", "value" : 3246.6 }
{ "_id" : "VA", "value" : 25.2 }
{ "_id" : "WA", "value" : 1964.9 }
sweetscomplete@fred-linux[up:214862]>
```

You can use the **$out** aggregation pipeline stage operator to output the results from `db.collection.aggregate()` into a separate collection.

Using the MongoDB Compass aggregation pipeline builder

The *MongoDB Compass* tool, introduced in `Chapter 1`, *Introducing MongoDB*, has an extremely useful feature which assists you in developing complex aggregation pipeline queries. To use Compass to build an aggregation pipeline query, you first need to start Compass and connect to MongoDB. You will then need to select the database and collection upon which you wish to perform an aggregation.

In the following example, we select the `sweetscomplete` database and the `purchases` collection. From the horizontal menu, we then select **Aggregations**. Here is how the screen appears so far:

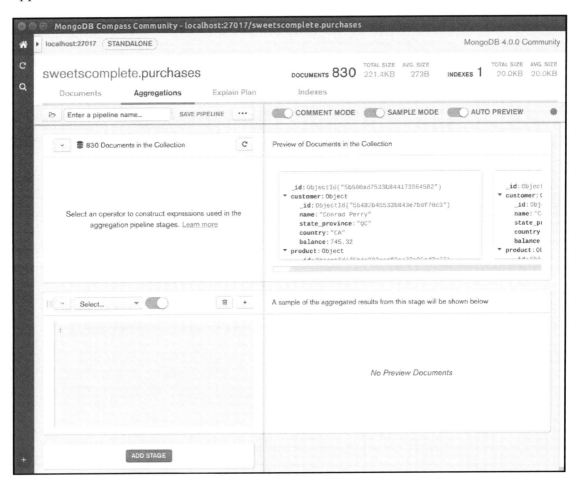

We then turn our attention to the dialog box in the bottom left. Clicking on **Select**, we add our first stage, $match. You can then start typing the start of the desired expression. The following tables summarizes possible initial actions:

If You Type ...	Compass Will Display a List Of ...
$	...expression operators allowed at this point
"	...fields you can use in the expression
[	... [ ], inside of which you will need to enter either $ or " to complete the array of expressions

In the following example, we wish to perform a match for all customers from Canada:

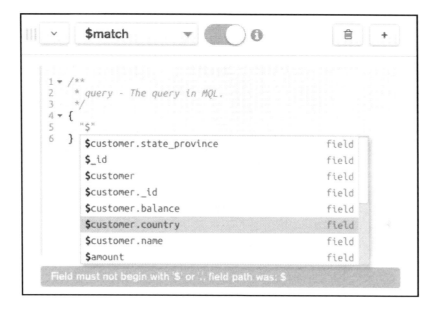

Once you have completed the arguments for a stage, you will see the results on the right, indicating the number of documents matched, with details on each document:

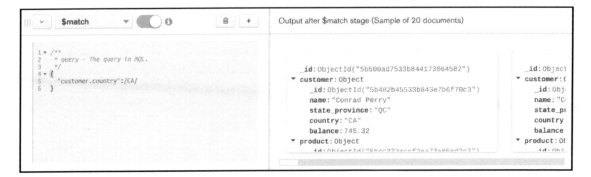

You are then free to add additional stages as desired. Once finished, queries can be retrieved, saved, and exported using the menu at the top left:

Summary

In this chapter, you learned how to conduct complex queries using the *aggregation pipeline* framework. You learned about stages, expression operators, and how to accumulate information such as sum, average, and so on. One of the most important aspects of the aggregation pipeline framework that you learned about in this chapter is the ability to access embedded objects or arrays.

You also learned about single-purpose aggregation (for example, sort and limit), as well as how to use map-reduce. You learned that, although map-reduce gives you flexibility in that JavaScript functions can be used, the aggregation framework is preferred as it uses native MongoDB methods and offers better performance.

In the next chapter, you will learn about how to maintain MongoDB performance.

6
Maintaining MongoDB Performance

The features covered in this chapter will show you how to improve performance by creating and using indexes, and how to safeguard data using replication and backups. In addition, you will learn how to handle massive amounts of data with sharding.

The topics that are going to be covered in this chapter are as follows:

- Indexes
- Simple backup and restore
- Replication
- Sharding

Indexes

Command summary:

```
db.collection.createIndex( { <fieldname> : ( 1 | -1 ) } );
```

Creating indexes is an easy way to improve MongoDB performance at the collection level. Indexes can be created on a single field, multiple fields, or embedded fields within arrays or objects. When you issue a query which involves the indexed field, MongoDB is able to use information stored in the index rather than having to do a full scan of all database documents. In this sense, you can think of the index as a shortcut which saves time when producing query results.

There are three index types supported by MongoDB: *single field* (https://docs.mongodb.com/manual/core/index-single/#single-field-indexes), *compound* (https://docs.mongodb.com/manual/core/index-compound/#compound-indexes), and *multi-key* (https://docs.mongodb.com/manual/core/index-multikey/#multikey-indexes).

Each of these can be defined as *ascending* or *descending*. In addition, there is an auto-generated default index on the `_id` field.

Single field indexes

For this illustration, we will use the `sweetscomplete.purchases` collection, which we described in `Chapter 5`, *Building Complex Queries Using Aggregation*. To avoid flipping pages, here is the first document in this collection to remind you of its structure:

```
Terminal
> db.purchases.findOne();
{
        "_id" : ObjectId("5b500ad7533b844173064582"),
        "customer" : {
                "_id" : ObjectId("5b482b45533b843e7b6f70c3"),
                "name" : "Conrad Perry",
                "state_province" : "QC",
                "country" : "CA",
                "balance" : 745.32
        },
        "product" : {
                "_id" : ObjectId("5b4c232accf2ea73a85ed2c7"),
                "sku" : "C22000",
                "title" : "Chocolate Toaster Tarts",
                "price" : 2.2
        },
        "date" : "2017-09-20",
        "quantity" : 15,
        "amount" : 33
}
>
```

Consider the following query:

```
db.purchases.find( {},
    {_id:0, date:1, "customer.name":1, "customer.country":1})
 .sort( {"customer.country":1, date:-1} );
```

If you frequently run queries which involve the `date` field, then it would improve the performance of `find()` and `sort()` to index this field. To create the index, you can use the collection method `createIndex()`, specifying the field on which to create the index as an argument. You would then use 1 for *ascending* and –1 for *descending*. The following example creates a descending index on the `date` field:

```
Terminal
> db.purchases.createIndex( { date: -1 } );
{
        "createdCollectionAutomatically" : false,
        "numIndexesBefore" : 1,
        "numIndexesAfter" : 2,
        "ok" : 1
}
> cls
```

You can also create single field indexes on embedded documents. In the following example, we are creating an ascending index on `customer.country`:

```
Terminal
> db.purchases.createIndex( { "customer.country": 1 } );
{
        "createdCollectionAutomatically" : false,
        "numIndexesBefore" : 2,
        "numIndexesAfter" : 3,
        "ok" : 1
}
>
```

> You can add the `explain("executionStats")` method to the cursor (for example, `db.collection.find().explain()`) to reveal performance statistics for your query before and after the index has been created.

Compound indexes

Compound indexes are useful when you wish to create an index on more than one field. To illustrate the use of this type of index, we will turn our attention again to the `sweetscomplete.purchases` collection. In this example, we issue a query which gives us a list of customers outside of the United States:

```
db.purchases.find(
    {"customer.country": {$not:/US/}},
{_id:0,"customer.name":1,"customer.state_province":1,"customer.country":1}
  ).sort(
    {"customer.country":1,"customer.state_province":1,"customer.name":1}
  );
```

When we tack the `explain("executionStats")` method to the query, we learn that this query takes 18 milliseconds to complete (only a fragment of the entire dump is shown):

```
"executionStats" : {
        "executionSuccess" : true,
        "nReturned" : 611,
        "executionTimeMillis" : 18,
        "totalKeysExamined" : 830,
        "totalDocsExamined" : 830,
```

We can now create an index on the fields that are included in the sort:

```
sweetscomplete@fred-linux[up:2861]>
db.purchases.createIndex(
...    {
...        "customer.country":1,
...        "customer.state_province":1,
...        "customer.name":1
...    }
... );
{
        "createdCollectionAutomatically" : false,
        "numIndexesBefore" : 1,
        "numIndexesAfter" : 2,
        "ok" : 1
}
sweetscomplete@fred-linux[up:2861]>
```

You will note that the execution time, after re-running the query, now takes 12 milliseconds (as shown in this fragment). It is worth mentioning that this is actually quite a significant speed improvement, given the small size of the collection. Imagine how much performance increase you would see on a large dataset!

```
"executionStats" : {
        "executionSuccess" : true,
        "nReturned" : 611,
        "executionTimeMillis" : 12,
        "totalKeysExamined" : 830,
        "totalDocsExamined" : 830,
```

Multi-key indexes

Multi-key indexes (https://docs.mongodb.com/manual/core/index-multikey/#multikey-indexes) are needed if you are dealing with documents with array fields. As an example, let's assume that sweetscomplete.customers now contains a new field called purch_history, with a list of purchase dates. We wish to generate a count of customers who have purchased items in June 2018. Granted we could generate the same information by scanning the purchases collection, but to illustrate the need for a multi-key index, let's examine this sample query:

```
db.customers.find( {
    purch_history: {
        $elemMatch: { $regex: /^2018-06/ }
    }
} ).count();
```

As you can see, from the query, the `purch_history` array is scanned using the `$elemMatch` array operator. To create the index, simply specify the field, in this case `purch_history`:

```
fred@fred-linux: ~/Desktop/Repos/MongoDB-Quick-Start-Guide-Doug
sweetscomplete@fred-linux[up:4532]> db.customers.createIndex( { purch_history: 1 } );
{
        "createdCollectionAutomatically" : false,
        "numIndexesBefore" : 1,
        "numIndexesAfter" : 2,
        "ok" : 1
}
sweetscomplete@fred-linux[up:4532]>
```

Simple backup and restore

Command summary (from the command line):

- `mongodump`
- `mongorestore`

Hopefully there is no need to stress how important it is to maintain a regular backup schedule. That being said, it is worth mentioning that doing a simple restore can actually cause problems in a properly constructed system of *replicas* or *shards* (covered later on in this chapter). In this section, we will address a simple backup of the MongoDB database that's residing on a single server.

mongodump

A backup can be as simple as issuing the command `mongodump`. This command will create a binary export of either a `mongod` or a `mongos` instance. Here is the output for the MongoDB instance, which is used to demonstrate concepts in this book:

```
fred@fred-linux: ~/Desktop/Repos/MongoDB-Quick-Start-Guide-Doug
fred@fred-linux:~/Desktop/Repos/MongoDB-Quick-Start-Guide-Doug$ mongodump
2018-08-05T20:29:39.040+0700    writing admin.system.version to
2018-08-05T20:29:39.041+0700    done dumping admin.system.version (1 document)
2018-08-05T20:29:39.041+0700    writing sweetscomplete.purchases to
2018-08-05T20:29:39.041+0700    writing sweetscomplete.customers to
2018-08-05T20:29:39.041+0700    writing sweetscomplete.products to
2018-08-05T20:29:39.042+0700    done dumping sweetscomplete.customers (76 documents)
2018-08-05T20:29:39.043+0700    done dumping sweetscomplete.products (64 documents)
2018-08-05T20:29:39.044+0700    done dumping sweetscomplete.purchases (830 documents)
fred@fred-linux:~/Desktop/Repos/MongoDB-Quick-Start-Guide-Doug$
```

There are a number of options available with this command. You can gain quick access to help by typing `mongodump --help`. The complete list is far too numerous to detail here, so we are including only certain key parameters, which are summarized in the following table. The options are switches which follow the `mongodump` command:

`-d <database>` | `--db=<database>`	Which database to dump.
`-c <collection>` | `--collection=<collection>`	Which collection to dump.
`-h <host>` | `--host=<host>`	Which host to connect to; if connecting to a replica set, use this syntax in place of `<host>`: `replSetName/host1:port, host2:port,` and so on. Where `replSetName` is the name of the replica set and `host` is the name of the host in the replica set. The `port` usually defaults to `27017`.

The following is an example of where we dump the `sweetscomplete` database and the `purchases` collection:

```
fred@fred-linux: ~/Desktop/Repos/MongoDB-Quick-Start-Guide-Doug
fred@fred-linux:~/Desktop/Repos/MongoDB-Quick-Start-Guide-Doug$
mongodump -d sweetscomplete -c purchases
2018-07-28T14:39:54.031+0700    writing sweetscomplete.purchases to
2018-07-28T14:39:54.036+0700    done dumping sweetscomplete.purchases (830 documents)
fred@fred-linux:~/Desktop/Repos/MongoDB-Quick-Start-Guide-Doug$
```

mongorestore

Restoring the database can be accomplished by issuing the command `mongorestore`. This command will import a binary export of either a `mongod` or a `mongos` instance. The command options you can use are the same as with `mongodump`, with these additions:

`-v`	Verbose: Gives you more information during the restore
`-dryRun`	Shows you what would happen if you actually performed the restore
`--drop`	Drops the collection before performing the restore

You can have a look here for more options regarding commands: `https://docs.mongodb.com/manual/reference/program/mongorestore/#mongorestore`.

In the following example, we are doing a *dry run* of restoring the `sweetscomplete.customers` collection to replicate the set `sweets_33`:

```
fred@fred-linux: ~/Desktop/Repos/MongoDB-Quick-Start-Guide-Doug
fred@fred-linux:~/Desktop/Repos/MongoDB-Quick-Start-Guide-Doug$
mongorestore -h sweets_33/ed:27017,fred:27017 -d sweetscomplete -c customers --drop -v -dryRun
./dump/sweetscomplete/customers.bson
2018-08-03T10:48:14.903+0700     using write concern: w='majority', j=false, fsync=false, wtimeout=0
2018-08-03T10:48:14.903+0700     checking for collection data in dump/sweetscomplete/customers.bson
2018-08-03T10:48:14.903+0700     found metadata for collection at dump/sweetscomplete/customers.metadata.json
2018-08-03T10:48:14.907+0700     dropping collection ryRun.customers before restoring
2018-08-03T10:48:14.952+0700     reading metadata for ryRun.customers from dump/sweetscomplete/customers.metadata.json
2018-08-03T10:48:14.952+0700     creating collection ryRun.customers using options from metadata
2018-08-03T10:48:14.985+0700     restoring ryRun.customers from dump/sweetscomplete/customers.bson
2018-08-03T10:48:15.375+0700     no indexes to restore
2018-08-03T10:48:15.375+0700     finished restoring ryRun.customers (76 documents)
2018-08-03T10:48:15.375+0700     done
fred@fred-linux:~/Desktop/Repos/MongoDB-Quick-Start-Guide-Doug$
```

Instead of specifying the *host*, *port*, and *database*, you can also use the `--uri` option, which lets you form a connection string that can also include the *username* and *password* if set.

Replication

Command summary:

- `rs.initiate( { _id: "<replicaSetName>", members: [ { _id: N, host: "<host>" } ] )`
- `rs.add( "<hostname>" | { host: "<hostname>" } )`
- `rs.remove( "<hostname>")`
- `rs.conf()`
- `rs.status()`

The purpose of replication is to provide immediate online redundancy so that there is no loss of service in case of failure. Before we get into the mechanics of how to create and use replicas, it's important to gain an understanding of what MongoDB replication is and how it operates.

Here are a couple of related topics which are beyond the scope of this book, but which might be of interest:

Change streams (`https://docs.mongodb.com/manual/changeStreams/#change-streams`) allows applications to subscribe to real-time changes in the data by using a Publish-Subscribe design.

Arbiters (`https://docs.mongodb.com/manual/core/replica-set-arbiter/index.html#replica-set-arbiter`) are voting members of the replica set which do not hold a copy of the data. They are used to *influence* elections.

Delayed replica set members (`https://docs.mongodb.com/manual/core/replica-set-delayed-member/#delayed-replica-set-members`) are servers which are part of a replica set, but which deliberately contain an older historic *snapshot* of the data, and can be used to recover from unsuccessful upgrades, operator errors, and so on.

Understanding MongoDB replication

A *replica set* is one or more MongoDB daemon instances, which we will refer to as *nodes*, with the same data. In order to maintain integrity, one of the nodes is *elected* (`https://docs.mongodb.com/manual/replication/#automatic-failover`) to intercept all reads and writes. This node is referred to as the *primary* (`https://docs.mongodb.com/manual/core/replica-set-primary/#replica-set-primary`). Changes to the database captured by the primary are then *replicated* to the secondaries by means of an *oplog* (`https://docs.mongodb.com/manual/core/replica-set-oplog/#replica-set-oplog`), which contains a list of operations to be applied:

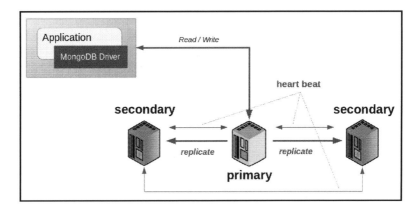

If the primary node fails to respond to the *heart beat*, an *election* occurs:

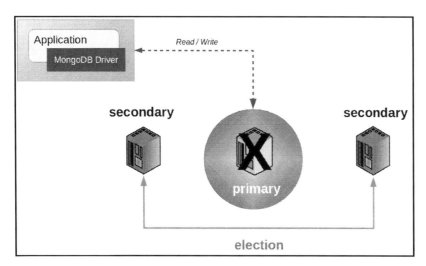

One of the secondaries is promoted to primary, and replication is able to continue unabated:

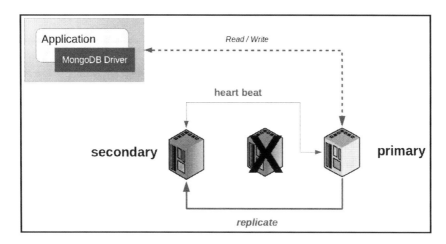

By default, an application reads from the *primary* in a replica set. This can cause bottlenecks in large distributed networks, and puts an undue load on the primary. Most read operations (for example, the db.collection.find() method) allow you to set the *read preference mode* (https://docs.mongodb.com/manual/core/read-preference/#read-preference-modes).

In order to control consistency and integrity when using replication, it would be of interest to become familiar with *read concerns* (https://docs. mongodb.com/manual/reference/read-concern/index.html#read-concern) and *write concerns* (https://docs.mongodb.com/manual/reference/write-concern/#write-concern). Read concerns allow you to set a parameter for a query whereby you indicate how rigorously you wish to guarantee the timeliness of the data. A write concern is the opposite: you can indicate what level of acknowledgement you wish to receive when writing critical data.

Deploying a replica set

The process of configuring and initializing the replica set is referred to in the MongoDB documentation as *deploying a replica set* (https://docs.mongodb.com/manual/tutorial/deploy-replica-set/#deploy-a-replica-set). There are four main steps involved:

- Backing up any data
- Configuring mongod to listen on an IP address which allows it to communicate with the other servers in the set
- Configuring mongod with a common name for the replica set
- Initializing the replica set

In the example we are going to illustrate in this section, the network is 192.168.2.0/24 and the replica set is sweets_33.

Resetting the IP address

Before you go through the process of creating a replica and deploying a replica set, you will need to reconfigure mongod to run on an IP address other than localhost (127.x.x.x). This can be accomplished by using the --bind_ip flag when starting mongod (where a.b.c.d is the target IP address):

```
mongod --bind_ip a.b.c.d
```

To bind to all IP addresses on this server, you can use this option:

```
mongod --bind_ip_all
```

The recommended approach is to modify the `mongod` configuration file on the impacted servers. Here are three possibilities:

If you want to have MongoDB listen with ...	Then enter this into the MongoDB config file
...a specific IP address, `a.b.c.d`	`net:` `    bindIp: a.b.c.d`
...only specific network interfaces, for example, `a.b.c.111` and `a.b.c.222`	`net:` `    bindIp: a.b.c.111,a.b.c.222`
...any (or all) IP addresses on the server	`net:` `    bindIp: 0.0.0.0`

You will then need to restart `mongod` using the `--config <filename>` option for this change to take effect. Please note that once you've changed `mongod` to listen to an IP address other than the default (localhost), you will need to enter this IP address when using the *mongo* shell, and any other tool which connects to `mongod` (for example, MongoDB Compass).

If you configure `mongod` to listen to any address other than localhost, it is vital that you first secure the database. See `Chapter 7`, *Securing MongoDB*, for more information.

Configuring the replica set member

In addition to resetting the IP address, each server which is a member of the replica set needs to be configured as such. As with the IP address binding, there are two ways to identify a server for the set. The first option is to use the following command-line flag when starting `mongod` (where XXX is the name of the replica set):

```
mongod --replSet "XXX"
```

Alternatively, you can add a configuration option to the `mongod` configuration file as follows:

```
replication:
    replSetName: "XXX"
```

You can then start `mongod` on each server in the replica set, as you would normally.

It is recommended that you should have three servers in a replica set, at a minimum. One will be the *primary*, the other two will be *secondaries*. Make sure that each server in the replica set can securely communicate with the others.

Initializing the replica set

The final step in the replica set's deployment is to open a *mongo* shell on *only one* of the servers in the replica set:

```
mongo --host <hostname>
```

You can then run the `rs.initiate()` command to perform the initialization. In the following example, we are initializing a replica set with three servers, ed, ted, and fred:

```
fred@fred-linux: ~/Desktop/Repos/MongoDB-Quick-Start-Guide-Doug
test@fred-linux[up:950]> rs.initiate( {
...      _id : "sweets_33",
...      members: [
...          { _id: 0, host: "ed" },
...          { _id: 1, host: "ted" },
...          { _id: 2, host: "fred" }
...      ]
... });
{
        "ok" : 1,
        "operationTime" : Timestamp(1532944427, 1),
        "$clusterTime" : {
                "clusterTime" : Timestamp(1532944427, 1),
                "signature" : {
                        "hash" : BinData(0,"AAAAAAAAAAAAAAAAAAAAAAAAAAA="),
                        "keyId" : NumberLong(0)
                }
        }
}
test@fred-linux[up:950]>
```

The `rs.conf()` and `rs.status()` commands can be used to confirm the status and health of the replica set. The full list of replica related commands can be found here: `https://docs.mongodb.com/manual/reference/method/js-replication/#replication-methods`.

Adding and removing members

Once you have a replica set up and running, over time, it will become necessary to add and remove members. This can be accomplished by reconfiguring the server so that it can be added or removed, and then issuing the appropriate command.

Removing a member from a replica set

To remove a member from a replica set, first shut down the mongod instance using the command for that operating system. For example, in Debian/Ubuntu Linux, issue the following command:

```
sudo service mongod stop
```

Then, from one of the servers remaining in the replica set, enter the *mongo* shell and run `rs.conf()` to find the hostname of the server to remove. You then execute `rs.remove( "<host>" )`, where `<host>` is exactly as shown from the output of `rs.conf()`:

```
fred@fred-linux: ~/Desktop/www/dr_tom/dentalwellness4u.com
test@fred-linux[up:170640]> rs.conf();
{
        "_id" : "sweets_33",
        "version" : 1,
        "protocolVersion" : NumberLong(1),
        "writeConcernMajorityJournalDefault" : true,
        "members" : [
                {
                        "_id" : 0,
                        "host" : "ed:27017",
                        "arbiterOnly" : false,
                        "buildIndexes" : true,
                        "hidden" : false,
                        "priority" : 1,
                        "tags" : {

                        },
                        "slaveDelay" : NumberLong(0),
                        "votes" : 1
                },
                {
                        "_id" : 1,
                        "host" : "ted:27017",
                        "arbiterOnly" : false,
                        "buildIndexes" : true,
                        "hidden" : false,
                        "priority" : 1,
                        "tags" : {
```

This forces a new *election*, and a new primary will be chosen from among the remaining members. You may have to restart the `mongod` instances on the remaining servers in the replica set to ensure full synchronization.

Adding a member to a replica set

The first consideration is to make sure that the proposed new member of the replica set is configured for the replica set it will join, and that its mongod instance is configured to listen on the correct IP address (see the section *Deploying a Replica Set*, for more information).

To add a member to a replica set, you will need to run a *mongo* shell from the primary. You can then issue the following command:

```
rs.add({ host: <hostname:port> });
```

Where hostname is the hostname, DNS, or IP address of the new server. The port will be 27017, or whatever port was assigned when MongoDB was installed on that server:

```
fred@fred-linux: ~/Desktop/www/dr_tom/dentalwellness4u.com
test@fred-linux[up:172410]> rs.add({ host: "ted:27017" });
{
        "ok" : 1,
        "operationTime" : Timestamp(1533116106, 1),
        "$clusterTime" : {
                "clusterTime" : Timestamp(1533116106, 1),
                "signature" : {
                        "hash" : BinData(0,"AAAAAAAAAAAAAAAAAAAAAAAAAAA="),
                        "keyId" : NumberLong(0)
                }
        }
}
```

If unsure which server is the primary server, run rs.status() on any server in the replica set and look at the value of the stateStr field for each server in the set.

Sharding

Command summary:

- sh.addShard("host:port")
- sh.enableSharding("database")
- sh.shardCollection("database.collection", { field: direction })
- sh.status()

Whereas *replication* is designed to provide redundancy of data, *sharding* is a feature which provides *horizontal scaling*. This means that instead of having a single extremely powerful server (*vertical scaling*), you spread the data across multiple servers operating in a cluster. This facility gives you the ability to handle massive amounts of data and lends itself to the cloud environment. Not only that, but because you have a subset of the entire database residing on multiple servers, each server is then able to handle its own database tasks, thus providing a means of *load balancing*.

Before we cover how to implement a *sharded cluster*, it's important to understand how sharding operates.

Understanding sharding

For the sake of illustration, we have a collection, X. Originally residing on a single server, we can create three shards and spread the collection across three servers. Each shard can be a *replica set* (which we discussed previously):

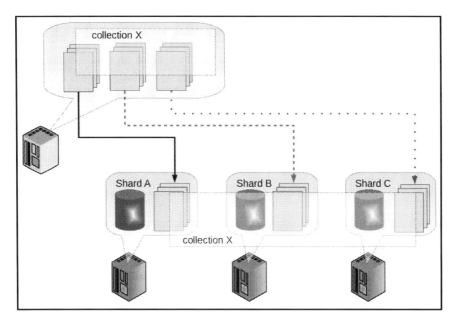

You would normally configure a **mongos (MongoDB shard routing service)** (`https://docs.mongodb.com/manual/core/sharded-cluster-query-router/#mongos`) instance to route reads and writes to specific shards in the cluster. The *mongos* instances are lightweight and can greatly enhance performance and scalability, especially when dealing with massive amounts of data. *Config servers* (`https://docs.mongodb.com/manual/core/sharded-cluster-config-servers/#config-servers`), which must be a replica set, are used to store metadata for a sharded cluster:

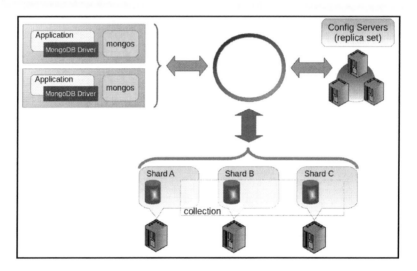

MongoDB sharding operates at the collection level. The collection is broken down into *chunks* (`https://docs.mongodb.com/manual/core/sharding-data-partitioning/#data-partitioning-with-chunks`), which are then distributed across the shards based on the *shard key* (`https://docs.mongodb.com/manual/core/sharding-shard-key/#shard-keys`). The configurable size limit of a chunk is 64 MB. The *sharded cluster balancer* (`https://docs.mongodb.com/manual/core/sharding-balancer-administration/#sharded-cluster-balancer`) is a background process which monitors each shard and ensures an even distribution of chunks between shards.

There are no specific restrictions on the size of the database which contains a sharded collection. A database can contain collections which are either sharded, non-sharded, or both. See the documentation on *sharded and non-sharded collections* (`https://docs.mongodb.com/manual/sharding/#sharded-and-non-sharded-collections`) for more information. There are certain minor operational restrictions on sharded clusters, however, which are summarized here: `https://docs.mongodb.com/manual/core/sharded-cluster-requirements/#operational-restrictions-in-sharded-clusters`.

The impact of sharding on performance becomes more and more evident as the amount of data to be processed increases. With sharding, read and write operations are spread across multiple servers which, not only positively impacts performance due to potentially parallel operations, but also, since the amount of data on any one server is reduced, performance improves.

Choosing a shard key

The *shard key* (`https://docs.mongodb.com/manual/sharding/#shard-keys`) is a document field (or fields) within the collection which forms the basis upon which MongoDB will distribute documents between the shards. This field (or fields) must be *immutable* (it cannot be changed once the document is saved), and must exist in every single document in the collection to be sharded. A collection can only have one shard key, and once chosen, cannot be changed. If no index for the shard key field exists, one is created automatically. The shard key is then used to determine how the chunks are created, which are then distributed across the shards.

Shard keys are chosen based on the following criteria:

- **Cardinality** (`https://en.wikipedia.org/wiki/Cardinality`): Number of elements in a set
- **Frequency** (`https://docs.mongodb.com/manual/core/sharding-shard-key/#shard-key-frequency`): How often this particular key appears in read/write operations
- **Change** (`https://docs.mongodb.com/manual/core/sharding-shard-key/#monotonically-changing-shard-keys`): How often the elements in the set change, and how often new elements are added to or removed from this set

The examples from the `customers` collection mentioned previously are for illustration only. The shard key needs to be immutable, thus if you choose `email` or `city` as your shard key, for example, and the customer changes their address, you could not change the value without doing a complete replace of the customer document.

Rather than using an existing field within a document for the shard key, you might consider creating a new field which could be a combination of some other fields so that it can become your new shard key.

Sharding strategies

There are two sharding strategies: *ranged* (`https://docs.mongodb.com/manual/core/ranged-sharding/#ranged-sharding`) and *hashed* (`https://docs.mongodb.com/manual/core/hashed-sharding/#hashed-sharding`). The choice of strategy depends, to a large extent, on the shard key chosen (see the preceding section for more information). Ideally, your choice of shard key and strategy will allow MongoDB to distribute documents evenly throughout the sharded cluster.

Ranged sharding

When using the ranged sharding strategy, which is the default, MongoDB distributes documents into chunks based on the value of the shard key. The chunks are then automatically distributed across the sharded cluster by the balancer.

In the following illustration, the shard key is X. Let's assume that the minimum value is 1, and the maximum is 100. Four ranges might be created: 0 to 24, 25 to 49, 50 to 74, and 75 to 100. When you write a document whose shard key, X, has a value of 24, it will be written to chunk 1. A document whose shard key value is 76 will end up in chunk 4:

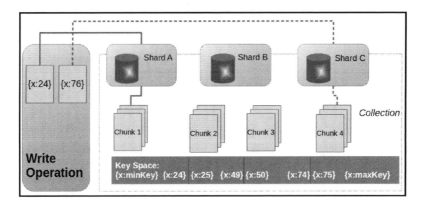

Use ranged sharding if your shard key has the following characteristics:

- High cardinality
- Low frequency
- Low change

Hashed sharding

The hashed sharding strategy creates a hash of the shard key before distributing documents between chunks:

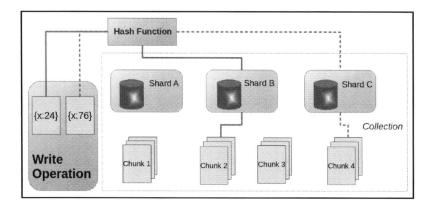

The advantage is that you are ensured an even distribution of data across shards. The disadvantage is that you lose the ability to target specific shards based on the knowledge of the contents of the shard key field.

Use hashed sharding if your shard key has either of the following characteristics:

- Low cardinality
- High change

Deploying a sharded cluster

In the following example, we are only using the configuration file option. If you are interested in the equivalent command-line options, see the tutorial on deploying a sharded cluster (`https://docs.mongodb.com/manual/tutorial/deploy-shard-cluster/#sharding-deploy-sharded-cluster`). Here is the list of servers that are used in this walkthrough:

- `ed` will be configured as a config server as part of replica set `config1`
- `fred` will host the `sweetscomplete` database and a shard from the `purchases` collection
- `zed` will host a shard from the `purchases` collection

Here are the steps to follow:

1. **Deploy the config server replica set**:
   Follow the same procedure that was outlined previously in the section on replication. The only difference is that you add an entry to the `mongod config` file `sharding:clusterRole:"configsvr"`, a part of which is shown here:

```
net:
    port: 27017
    bindIp: 0.0.0.0

replication:
    replSetName: "config1"

sharding:
    clusterRole: "configsvr"
```

You will also need to initialize the replica set (as described in the section on *Replication*):

```
> rs.initiate(
...    {
...        _id: "config1",
...        configsvr: true,
...        members: [ { _id:0, host:"ed" } ]
...    }
... );
{
        "ok" : 1,
        "operationTime" : Timestamp(1533356344, 1),
        "$gleStats" : {
                "lastOpTime" : Timestamp(1533356344, 1),
                "electionId" : ObjectId("000000000000000000000000")
        },
        "lastCommittedOpTime" : Timestamp(0, 0),
        "$clusterTime" : {
                "clusterTime" : Timestamp(1533356344, 1),
                "signature" : {
                        "hash" : BinData(0,"AAAAAAAAAAAAAAAAAAAAAAAAAAA="),
                        "keyId" : NumberLong(0)
                }
        }
}
config1:OTHER>
```

2. **Choose (or create) the shard key within the collection to be sharded**:
For the purposes of this illustration, the collection to be sharded will be
`sweetscomplete.purchases`. We will choose the `date` field as our hash key.
Because the date is ever increasing, this means it has high *cardinality*. Also, since
any given date is unlikely to appear in a query with a large number of times, it
has low *frequency*. This might lead us to choose the *ranged* sharding strategy.
Since dates are ever increasing, however, we risk bottlenecks in the shard, which
has the maximum key. The benefit we gain by having specific knowledge of the
date and being able to target specific shards in our queries makes the *ranged*
strategy more attractive.

3. **Deploy the shard replica sets**:
For each server which will host a shard, add the config option
`sharding:clusterRole:"shardsvr"` to its `mongod config` file.
You can then restart `mongod` on each server. If you are configuring shards on
replica sets, connect to one of the servers in the set (for example, the primary),
and initialize it using `rs.initiate()`, like we described previously. In a
production environment, it is highly recommended that you configure a replica
set for each shard.

4. **Connect a mongos to the sharded cluster**:
The *mongos* instance acts as a router for queries to sharded clusters. You can run
it on any server which is accessible by the cluster. In the following example, we
are running it on the *config server*. Like the `mongod` daemon itself, *mongos* can
have a configuration file. Note that you need to specify a port for the config
server, and a different port for *mongos*. Here is the example we are using:

- We then start *mongos* using the `--config` option, in this case to `/etc/mongos.conf`: Note that you need to assign the appropriate permissions so that the mongos user is able to open the TCP port specified in the configuration file:

```
mongos --config /etc/mongos.conf
```

- Finally, to perform the next two steps, use the *mongo* shell to connect to the *mongos* instance instead of *mongod*:

```
fred@fred-linux: ~
fred@fred-linux:~$ mongo --host ed:27019
MongoDB shell version v4.0.0
connecting to: mongodb://ed:27019/
MongoDB server version: 4.0.0
Server has startup warnings:
2018-08-05T05:42:47.492+0100 I CONTROL  [main]
2018-08-05T05:42:47.492+0100 I CONTROL  [main] ** WARNING: Access control is
not enabled for the database.
2018-08-05T05:42:47.492+0100 I CONTROL  [main] **          Read and write acc
ess to data and configuration is unrestricted.
2018-08-05T05:42:47.492+0100 I CONTROL  [main] ** WARNING: You are running th
is process as the root user, which is not recommended.
2018-08-05T05:42:47.492+0100 I CONTROL  [main]
test@ed:27019[up:1244]>
```

5. **Add shards to the cluster**:
   In order to add shards to the cluster, from the *mongo* shell, we need to connect to the *mongos* instance. We then issue the command `sh.addShard( "host:port" )` until all of the shards have been added:

```
fred@fred-linux: ~
test@ed:27019[up:1025]> sh.addShard("fred:27017");
{
        "shardAdded" : "shard0000",
        "ok" : 1,
        "operationTime" : Timestamp(1533445224, 6),
        "$clusterTime" : {
                "clusterTime" : Timestamp(1533445224, 6),
                "signature" : {
                        "hash" : BinData(0,"AAAAAAAAAAAAAAAAAAAAAAAAAAA="),
                        "keyId" : NumberLong(0)
                }
        }
}
test@ed:27019[up:1025]>
```

6. **Enable sharding for the database**:
   Still connected via the *mongo* shell to the *mongos* instance, we enable sharding for the database using the command `sh.enableSharding( "database")`:

```
fred@fred-linux: ~
test@ed:27019[up:1244]> sh.enableSharding( "sweetscomplete" );
{
        "ok" : 1,
        "operationTime" : Timestamp(1533445840, 3),
        "$clusterTime" : {
                "clusterTime" : Timestamp(1533445840, 3),
                "signature" : {
                        "hash" : BinData(0,"AAAAAAAAAAAAAAAAAAAAAAAAAAA="),
                        "keyId" : NumberLong(0)
                }
        }
}
test@ed:27019[up:1244]>
```

7. **Shard the collection using either the ranged or hashed sharding strategies**:
   As mentioned previously, there are two sharding strategies to choose from. In our example, we will use the *ranged* strategy. First, we create an index on the shard key, which in this illustration is the `date` field, using the following command:

   db.purchases.createIndex({ date: 1 });

8. We then use the command `sh.shardCollection( "database.collection", { field: direction } )` to complete the operation. Note that if you wish to use *hashed* sharding, substitute `"hashed"` in place of *direction*:

```
fred@fred-linux: ~
sweetscomplete@ed:27019[up:1244]>
sh.shardCollection("sweetscomplete.purchases", { date: 1 } );
{
        "collectionsharded" : "sweetscomplete.purchases",
        "collectionUUID" : UUID("cfe9f701-ae26-46ef-ad0e-7b408901bf47"),
        "ok" : 1,
        "operationTime" : Timestamp(1533446408, 8),
        "$clusterTime" : {
                "clusterTime" : Timestamp(1533446408, 8),
                "signature" : {
                        "hash" : BinData(0,"AAAAAAAAAAAAAAAAAAAAAAAAAAA="),
                        "keyId" : NumberLong(0)
                }
        }
}
sweetscomplete@ed:27019[up:1244]>
```

The `sh.status()` command gives us an overview on the sharding process:

```
fred@fred-linux: ~
sweetscomplete@ed:27019[up:1244]> sh.status();
--- Sharding Status ---
  sharding version: {
        "_id" : 1,
        "minCompatibleVersion" : 5,
        "currentVersion" : 6,
        "clusterId" : ObjectId("5b65293a7871cf9e665a7a5b")
  }
  shards:
        {  "_id" : "shard0000",  "host" : "fred:27017",  "state" : 1 }
        {  "_id" : "shard0001",  "host" : "zed:27017",  "state" : 1 }
  active mongoses:
        "4.0.0" : 1
  autosplit:
        Currently enabled: yes
  balancer:
        Currently enabled:  yes
        Currently running:  no
        Failed balancer rounds in last 5 attempts:  0
        Migration Results for the last 24 hours:
                No recent migrations
  databases:
        {  "_id" : "config",  "primary" : "config",  "partitioned" : true }
                config.system.sessions
                        shard key: { "_id" : 1 }
                        unique: false
                        balancing: true
                        chunks:
                                shard0000       1
                        { "_id" : { "$minKey" : 1 } } -->> { "_id" : { "$maxKey" : 1 }
} on : shard0000 Timestamp(1, 0)
        {  "_id" : "sweetscomplete",  "primary" : "shard0000",  "partitioned" : true,
"version" : {  "uuid" : UUID("f0849cc0-a79c-4747-8215-0ae0515eef90"),  "lastMod" : 1
} }
```

Before you deploy a sharded cluster, make sure that all of the involved servers can communicate securely. If you experience connection errors during the deployment process, the first thing to check is your firewall settings.

Summary

In this chapter, you learned about maintenance and performance. You first learned about simple backup and restore using `mongodump` and `mongorestore`. You then went on to learn about creating indexes, including single field, multiple field, and multi-key. After that, you learned about replica sets, that is, primary and secondaries, how to deploy them, and adding or removing members. Finally, you learned about sharding, config servers, shard servers, range and hashed sharding strategies, and how to choose a shard key.

In the next chapter, you will learn various security-related considerations, in addition to learning how to secure a MongoDB database.

7
Securing MongoDB

This chapter explains how to secure the database itself, add users, and adjust permissions to specific collections. You will also learn how to enforce authentication and create an admin user. In addition, we will address how to configure MongoDB to use SSL/TLS.

The topics that are going to be covered in this chapter are as follows:

- MongoDB security overview
- Transport Layer Security
- Authentication
- Access control

MongoDB security overview

By default, after first installing the MongoDB database, there will be no security. Unlike earlier versions, however, as of MongoDB version 4.0, `mongod` binds to *localhost*, which provides a limited measure of safety. This lack of security facilitates initial administration and development. A production server, of course, will need a full measure of security.

Before deploying any measures (for example, replication or sharding) which would cause the database to be exposed to the company network, you should first implement proper security measures. MongoDB security encompasses several aspects, all of which are covered in this chapter. These include transport layer security, authentication, and access control.

The basic checklist for establishing security is as follows:

- Configuring MongoDB for **TLS** (**Transport Layer Security**)
- Defining the authentication mechanism infrastructure (SCRAM, x.509 certificates, and so on)
- Creating the *admin* user, thereby enabling access control and enforcing authentication
- If you need to, defining roles with specific sets of privilege actions
- Creating database users that are going to be assigned to one or more roles

Other considerations not covered in this book include encrypting sensitive data, limiting exposure to the internet, and performing regular security audits. We will start our discussion by covering TLS.

Transport Layer Security

Contrary to what you would expect from its name, *Transport Layer Security* (https://en.wikipedia.org/wiki/Transport_Layer_Security) does not concern the **TCP** (**Transmission Control Protocol**) layer of the TCP/IP protocol stack. Instead, TLS in this context applies to the *application* (https://en.wikipedia.org/wiki/Application_layer) (top) layer. The data at this layer is transmitted using end-to-end encryption based on a *secret* which the sender and receiver share, thus ensuring the privacy of the communication. In addition, depending on how the protocol is configured, one or both sides can be authenticated, and a message integrity check can be enabled to ensure the reliability of the message.

Two protocols are used to ensure transport layer security: **SSL** (**Secure Sockets Layer**) and TLS . Of the two, only TLS should be used, and even at that, the later the version, the better. TLS v1.3 was published on 10th August 2018 as RFC 8446 (https://tools.ietf.org/html/rfc8446), which would be the best current choice, however it might not be supported by your operating system.

A discussion of algorithms, ciphers, and modes is beyond the scope of this book, however it's worth noting that **AES** (**Advanced Encryption Standard**, also known as *Rijndael*, https://en.wikipedia.org/wiki/Advanced_Encryption_Standard), Camellia (https://en.wikipedia.org/wiki/Camellia_(cipher)), and ARIA (https://en.wikipedia.org/wiki/ARIA_(cipher)) ciphers using **GCM** (**Galois Counter Mode**, https://en.wikipedia.org/wiki/Galois/Counter_Mode) have been tested as the most secure at the time of writing.

Changes in MongoDB v4.0

As of MongoDB v4.0, several significant transport layer security changes have been made: TLS 1.0 is no longer supported if TLS 1.1 or above is available due to serious security vulnerabilities that were uncovered in TLS 1.0. Another change is that MongoDB v4.0 now uses the following native TLS/SSL libraries:

Operating System	TLS/SSL Library
Windows	Secure Channel (`https://docs.microsoft.com/en-us/windows/desktop/SecAuthN/secure-channel`)
Linux/BSD	OpenSSL (`https://www.openssl.org/`)
Mac OS X	Secure Transport (`https://developer.apple.com/documentation/security/secure_transport`)

Another change introduced in MongoDB v4.0 is the ability to retrieve keys and certificates from *system stores* when running on Mac or Windows. This is an alternative to using PEM key files (which we will describe shortly). In order to take advantage of this feature, you need to decide upon a *certificate selector* (`https://docs.mongodb.com/manual/reference/program/mongod/#cmdoption-mongod-sslcertificateselector`). Selectors can be either of the following:

- **Subject**: The distinguished name (`https://www.ietf.org/rfc/rfc4514.txt`) of the *subject*, as stated in the certificate
- **Thumbprint**: A string of bytes in hexadecimal which represents the SHA-1 digest of a public key, also referred to as the *fingerprint*

To invoke the certificate selector feature, you can start the `mongod` instance using the following command-line option:

```
--sslCertificateSelector <subject|thumbprint>=<value>
```

Alternatively, just add the following to the MongoDB `config` file:

```
net:
    ssl:
        certificateSelector: <subject|thumbprint>=<value>
```

 The `certificateSelector` and `PEMKeyFile` directives are mutually exclusive: use one or the other, but not both!

x.509 certificates

In order to use TLS, you need to either acquire or generate certificates for your servers and clients. In a production environment, these would be signed by a **Certificate Authority (CA)** (https://en.wikipedia.org/wiki/Certificate_authority). There are a number of commercial organizations that provide this service (for a fee, of course!), including IdenTrust (https://identrust.com/), Comodo (https://www.comodo.com/), and DigiCert (https://www.digicert.com/). Another way to obtain a signed certificate might be through internet service providers, who often include a digital certificate in their offerings. Finally, consider using free open source certificate authorities, including *Let's Encrypt* (https://letsencrypt.org/), which is sponsored by Mozilla, Cisco, **EFF (Electronic Frontier Foundation)**, and GitHub, among others.

For the purposes of this demonstration, we will use a locally generated self-signed certificate (https://stackoverflow.com/questions/10175812/how-to-create-a-self-signed-certificate-with-openssl). The demonstration system is Ubuntu Linux 18.04. We will proceed as follows:

1. Open a terminal window as a root user.
2. Generate a key and self-signed certificate request. Enter a *passphrase* to provide encryption:

```
openssl genrsa -des3 -out ca.key 4096
openssl req -new -x509 -days 365 -key ca.key -out ca.crt
cat ca.key ca.crt >ca.pem
```

```
root@zed: /etc/ssl
File Edit View Search Terminal Help
root@zed:/etc/ssl# openssl req -new -x509 -days 365 -key ca.key -out ca.crt
Enter pass phrase for ca.key:
You are about to be asked to enter information that will be incorporated
into your certificate request.
What you are about to enter is what is called a Distinguished Name or a DN.
There are quite a few fields but you can leave some blank
For some fields there will be a default value,
If you enter '.', the field will be left blank.
-----
Country Name (2 letter code) [AU]:TH
State or Province Name (full name) [Some-State]:Surin
Locality Name (eg, city) []:Surin
Organization Name (eg, company) [Internet Widgits Pty Ltd]:unlikelysource.com
Organizational Unit Name (eg, section) []:mongodb
Common Name (e.g. server FQDN or YOUR name) []:cn=zed,ou=mongodb,dc=unlikelysou
rce,dc=com
Email Address []:doug@unlikelysource.com
root@zed:/etc/ssl#
```

3. Create a key, a certificate signing request that's signed by the self-signed CA, and a PEM file for the `mongod` instance:

```
openssl genrsa -des3 -out mongod.key 4096
openssl req -new -key mongod.key -out mongod.csr
openssl x509 -req -days 365 -in mongod.csr -CA ca.crt \
  -CAkey ca.key -set_serial 01 -out mongod.crt
cat mongod.key mongod.crt >mongod.pem
```

4. It's important to note that we created an entry in `/etc/hosts` for `mongod` and assigned it the IP address of the server. When asked for the *Common Name*, instead of entering an x.509 *distinguished name*, we simply entered `mongod`.

5. Do the same for the client. In this example, the client is `zed`:

```
openssl genrsa -des3 -out zed.key 4096
openssl req -new -key zed.key -out zed.csr
openssl x509 -req -days 365 -in zed.csr -CA ca.crt \
  -CAkey ca.key -set_serial 01 -out zed.crt
cat zed.key zed.crt > zed.pem
```

6. Due to performing the preceding step, we created an entry in `/etc/hosts` for `zed` and entered `zed` as the *Common Name*.

At this point, we have three `*.key` (keys), three `*.crt` (certificates), and two `*.csr` (certificate signing request) files in the `/etc/ssl` directory and also three `*.pem` files..

 CA stands for **certificate authority** (`https://en.wikipedia.org/wiki/Certificate_authority`) and **PEM** stands for **privacy enhanced mail** (`https://en.wikipedia.org/wiki/Privacy-Enhanced_Mail`).

Configuring mongod to use TLS

Certificates in hand, we are now ready to start our `mongod` **instance** using TLS. Add the following options to the MongoDB `config` file, or add the equivalent command-line parameters when starting the `mongod` instance:

MongoDB Config File Entry	Command Line Parameter	Value
`net.ssl.mode`	`--sslMode`	`requireSSL`
`net.ssl.PEMKeyFile`	`--sslPEMKeyFile`	`/path/to/PEM/file/for/server`
`net.ssl.CAFile`	`--sslCAFile`	`/path/to/CA/PEM/file`
`net.ssl.PEMKeyPassword`	`--sslPEMKeyPassword`	`"password"` (only if encrypted)

Here is a fragment concerning TLS taken from the `/etc/mongod.conf` file of the demo system:

```
net:
  port: 27017
  bindIp: 0.0.0.0
  ssl:
    mode: requireSSL
    PEMKeyFile: /etc/ssl/mongod.pem
    PEMKeyPassword: "password"
    CAFile: /etc/ssl/ca.pem
```

Authentication

Authentication is the process of determining *are you who you say you are?*. Authentication is not required until you enable access control (covered in the next section). At first, it might appear that authentication and access control are the same thing. They are both aspects of security, but authentication occurs **before** access control. In other words, MongoDB needs to first confirm *you are who you say you are* before deciding what actions you are allowed to perform.

Authentication itself takes different forms. In one case, you might be a user who wishes to run commands via the *mongo* shell. Another case would be a series of database commands being issued by an application using a MongoDB programming language driver. There is yet a third form of authentication whereby you can configure authentication between servers in a replica set or a sharded cluster (see `Chapter 6`, *Maintaining MongoDB Performance*).

MongoDB supports four authentication mechanisms. The first two are available in the Community Edition. The last two are only available in the Enterprise (paid) Edition:

- SCRAM
- x.509 Certificate
- Kerberos
- **LDAP (Lightweight Directory Access Protocol)**

SCRAM

SCRAM (Salted Challenge-Response Authentication Mechanism, `https://docs.` `mongodb.com/manual/core/security-scram/#scram`) is the default authentication mechanism. This mechanism provides several options, including the ability to provide a unique *salt* per user. This greatly enhances randomization and can potentially limit damage if one user account is compromised. In addition, you can adjust the *iteration count*, also referred to as *cost*. The higher the cost, the harder it is to crack the password. The trade-off is that it takes longer to generate the hash.

The two SCRAM algorithms supported are summarized as follows:

- **SCRAM-SHA-1**:
  SHA-1 (Secure Hash Algorithm 1, `https://en.wikipedia.org/wiki/SHA-1`) was introduced by the United States **National Security Agency (NSA)** in 1995. Since that time, it is no longer considered secure against brute-force attacks. Furthermore, in 2017, Google announced that they had successfully launched a *collision attack* whereby the same hash was produced by two different files, which is bad news if you want to have a secure password. Nonetheless, if you're stuck with this algorithm, you can at least increase the cost. The default is 10000. Add this parameter when connecting to either `mongod` or `mongos`:

  ```
  --setParameter scramIterationCount=<cost>
  ```

- **SCRAM-SHA-256**:
  SHA-256 (`https://en.wikipedia.org/wiki/SHA-2`), also developed by the NSA, was first published in 2001. Although exhibiting a greatly enhanced resistance to *collision* attacks from which SHA-1 suffers, it is still vulnerable to *pseudo-collision* and *length extension* attacks.
  Even so, as with the MongoDB SCRAM-SHA-1 algorithm, you can at least increase the cost. The default is 15000. Add this parameter when connecting to either `mongod` or `mongos`:

  ```
  --setParameter scramSHA256IterationCount=<cost>
  ```

As of MongoDB v4.0, MongoDB-CR (Challenge Reponse) is no longer supported. If you wish to migrate your database from an earlier version of MongoDB to v4.0, you **must** update these credentials to SCRAM *before* performing the MongoDB upgrade.

Mongo shell authentication using SCRAM

To authenticate as a user using the *mongo* shell, you can use the command-line parameters that are summarized here:

Short Syntax	Long Syntax
-u <username>	--username <username>
-p [<password>]	--password [<password>]

If you do not specify a password but use the -p or --password flag, you will be prompted for the password interactively. You will also need to add the following parameter if the database in which the user created is not the one you wish to connect to:

```
--authenticationDatabase <dbname>
```

Internal communication using SCRAM

In order to secure communications between members of a replica set or sharded cluster, you need to create a *keyfile* (https://docs.mongodb.com/manual/core/security-internal-authentication/#keyfiles). The keyfile will then need to be copied to each member of the set or cluster. The length of each key can be from 6 to 1,024 characters, and can include any character defined in RFC 4648, base64 encoding (https://tools.ietf.org/html/rfc4648#section-4). You can then restart each member mongod instance after adding the following to its MongoDB config file:

```
security:
    keyFile: <path/to/key/file>
```

Alternatively, you can restart the mongod instance with the following command-line switch:

```
--keyFile <path-to-keyfile>
```

Do not use SCRAM keyfile security for a production environment. Use x.509 certificates, or upgrade to the MongoDB Enterprise Edition and use Kerberos (covered later).

x.509 authentication

MongoDB support for x.509 certificates offers an alternative approach for authentication. x.509 (`https://en.wikipedia.org/wiki/X.509`) is an internationally recognized standard which defines *public key certificates* issued by *trusted certificate authorities* (`https://en.wikipedia.org/wiki/Certificate_authority`) that are used to encrypt a message, and mathematically related *private keys* which are used to decrypt the message. This forms the basis of HTTPS as well as TLS and **SSL** (**Secure S0ckets Layer**).

In order to use x.509 certificates, you need to configure MongoDB to use SSL/TLS (see the *Transport Security Layer* section for more details). If you wish to allow users to authenticate using unique x.509 user certificates, you will need to add the following to the MongoDB config file (this assumes that you also want to continue with plain text and SCRAM authentication locally):

```
setParameter:
    authenticationMechanisms: PLAIN,SCRAM-SHA-256,MONGODB-X509
```

Mongo shell authentication using x.509

In order to use x.509 certificates for *mongo* shell authentication, you must have access to a valid Certificate Authority, and a signed certificate available. In addition, you will need to generate a unique certificate for each user. To authenticate the *mongo* shell, use the command-line parameters shown here. Note that the hostname needs to match the one that's in the x.509 certificate:

```
mongo --ssl --sslPEMKeyFile </client/PEM/file> --sslCAFile </CA/PEM/file> --host "<matches cert>"
```

In the following example, we use the `/etc/ssl/zed.pem` file that we showed you earlier in this chapter:

```
                                        zed@zed: ~
 File  Edit  View  Search  Terminal  Help
zed@zed:~$ mongo  --ssl -sslPEMKeyFile /etc/ssl/client.pem --sslPEMKeyPassword "password" --sslCAFile /etc/ssl/ca.pem --host mongod
MongoDB shell version v4.0.0
connecting to: mongodb://mongod:27017/
MongoDB server version: 4.0.0
Server has startup warnings:
2018-08-19T14:29:10.614+0700 I STORAGE  [initandlisten]
2018-08-19T14:29:10.614+0700 I STORAGE  [initandlisten] ** WARNING: Using the XFS filesystem is strongly recommended with the WiredT
iger storage engine
2018-08-19T14:29:10.614+0700 I STORAGE  [initandlisten] **          See http://dochub.mongodb.org/core/prodnotes-filesystem
2018-08-19T14:29:15.159+0700 I CONTROL  [initandlisten]
2018-08-19T14:29:15.159+0700 I CONTROL  [initandlisten] ** WARNING: Access control is not enabled for the database.
2018-08-19T14:29:15.159+0700 I CONTROL  [initandlisten] **          Read and write access to data and configuration is unrestricted.
2018-08-19T14:29:15.159+0700 I CONTROL  [initandlisten]
---
Enable MongoDB's free cloud-based monitoring service to collect and display
metrics about your deployment (disk utilization, CPU, operation statistics,
etc).

The monitoring data will be available on a MongoDB website with a unique
URL created for you. Anyone you share the URL with will also be able to
view this page. MongoDB may use this information to make product
improvements and to suggest MongoDB products and deployment options to you.

To enable free monitoring, run the following command:
db.enableFreeMonitoring()
---
>
```

Internal authentication using x.509

In order to establish secure internal communications between members of a replica set or sharded cluster, you need to issue x.509 certificates (`https://www.ietf.org/rfc/rfc5280.txt`) from the same **Certificate Authority (CA)**. Furthermore, the certificate's *subject* must consist of the following:

- A **Common Name (CN)**
- Any (or a combination) of the following:
  - **Organizational Unit (OU)**
  - **Organization (O)**
  - **Domain Component (DC)**

The CN must be unique for each certificate for each member. The combination of OU, O, and DC must be the same. Thus, if you have three servers, ed, ned, and zed, in a replica set, the subject for each server's certificate might appear as follows:

```
subject= CN=ed,ou=sales,o=London,dc=sweetscomplete,dc=com
subject= CN=ned,ou=sales,o=London,dc=sweetscomplete,dc=com
subject= CN=zed,ou=sales,o=London,dc=sweetscomplete,dc=com
```

You then restart each mongod instance using the following command-line options:

```
mongod --sslMode requireSSL --sslPEMKeyFile </path> --sslCAFile </path> --
clusterAuthMode x509
```

Even better, include the equivalent directives in the MongoDB config file as follows:

```
security:
    clusterAuthMode: x509
 net:
    ssl:
        mode: requireSSL
        PEMKeyFile: <path/to/TLS/SSL/certificate/key/PEM/file>
        CAFile: <path/to/root/CA/PEM/file>
    bindIp: 0.0.0.0
```

Kerberos

The MongoDB *Enterprise* edition offers two additional authentication mechanisms: *kerberos* and *LDAP*. Kerberos originated at **MIT (Massachusetts Institute of Technology)** as part of a larger project in the mid 1980s. Version 5 was published in 1993 and appeared in the public domain as RFC 1510 (https://tools.ietf.org/html/rfc1510), which was later superseded by RFC 4120 (https://tools.ietf.org/html/rfc4120) in 2005. Interestingly, as of Windows 2000 (https://en.wikipedia.org/wiki/Windows_2000), Microsoft adopted Kerberos as its default authentication mechanism, and has made significant contributions to the protocol.

Every node in the Kerberos authentication scheme is referred to as a *principal*, and must have a unique name. To facilitate scalability, principals are assigned to *realms*, each of which has its own **KDC (Kerberos key distribution center)**. This is much like a replica set which consists of members, one of which is the primary.

The following diagram summarizes the exchange which takes place when a client makes an authentication request for a service. **TGS** stands for **Ticket Granting Service**:

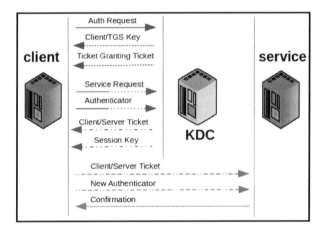

To configure MongoDB Enterprise edition for Kerberos, proceed as follows:

1. Start the `mongod` instance without Kerberos and connect using the *mongo* shell.

2. Add *principals* to the `$external` database (authentication database) by using the following command:

```
db.createUser( {
    user: "<principal>@<REALM>",
    roles: [ { role: "<role>", db: "<database name>" } ]
} );
```

Where *principal* could take either of these forms:

```
<username>@<REALM> or <servicename>/<instance>@<REALM>
```

3. Linux only: Set the environment variable `KRB5_KTNAME` to the keytab file (`https://docs.mongodb.com/manual/core/kerberos/#linux-keytab-files`) path (the file which contains the Kerberos keys).

4. Start `mongod` with Kerberos support by adding the following command-line option:

```
--authenticationMechanism=GSSAPI
```

5. As well as the following option if the hostname doesn't match the Kerberos name:

```
--gssapiHostName <alt hostname>
```

LDAP

LDAP stands for *lightweight directory access protocol* and is precisely defined in RFC 4511 (`https://tools.ietf.org/html/rfc4511`). The protocol evolved as a spin-off from the more comprehensive (but ultimately unwieldy) `x.500` **DAP (Directory Access Protocol)** that was produced by a consortium of telecommunications companies known as the **ITU (International Telecommunication Union)** in concert with **ISO (International Standards Organization)** in the 1980s. Simply put, the original idea was to provide a global digital equivalent of the traditional *phone book*, which is bulky, expensive to produce and distribute, and generally out of date the moment it's printed.

Because the X.500 specifications were so unwieldy, and were further complicated by conflicting implementations schemes promoted by vested interests, a *lightweight* version was introduced in 1993. LDAP, as it became known, is much less ambitious in scope, but much more workable. It was designed to allow access to an X.500-based digital directory, and uses much less bandwidth than other existing and now obsolete directory access protocols. The current version, v3, was published in 2006 as RFC 4511 by an engineering team working for Novell, Inc. MongoDB only supports authentication via LDAP in the Enterprise Edition.

To configure MongoDB to authenticate via LDAP, you must add the `security.ldap.servers` directive to the MongoDB `config` file:

```
security:
    ldap:
        servers: "host1:port"[,"host2:port",etc.]
```

Other optional parameters are identified in the documentation reference for *LDAP Authentication via Operating System LDAP Libraries* (`https://docs.mongodb.com/manual/core/security-ldap/#ldap-authentication-via-the-operating-system-ldap-libraries`).

If you are running MongoDB on a Linux server, you also have the option of authenticating via the SASL daemon `saslauthd`. Note that this options is not available for MongoDB instances running on Windows servers. Add the following to the MongoDB `config` file:

```
security:
    authorization: enabled
  setParameter:
    authenticationMechanisns: PLAIN
    saslauthdPath: /path/to/saslauthd
```

MongoDB can use any LDAP compliant server as an authentication source, including the following:

- Microsoft Active Directory (`https://docs.microsoft.com/en-us/windows-server/identity/ad-ds/get-started/virtual-dc/active-directory-domain-services-overview`)
- OpenLDAP (`http://www.openldap.org/`)
- NetIQ eDirectory (formerly Novell eDirectory, `https://www.netiq.com/documentation/edirectory-91/`)

Access control

Access control (also referred to as *authorization*) defines and enforces what actions a database user is allowed to perform once authenticated. Access control follows authentication: you cannot have one without the other! As you may recall from our previous discussion, *authentication* is the process of determining the identity of a user. Access control, on the other hand, determines what the user can do.

You establish access control over one or more databases by assigning *privilege actions* (`https://docs.mongodb.com/manual/reference/privilege-actions/#privilege-actions`) to roles. Privileges fall into three general categories: **CRUD (Create Read Update Delete)** operations, Database Management (for example, managing database users), and Infrastructure Management (for example, replication and sharding operations).

Initializing security

Setting up initial security in MongoDB is actually an extremely simple operation. Here are the steps that need to be performed:

- Start the `mongod` instance with no security.
- Access the database using the *mongo* shell or an admin tool such as MongoDB Compass.
- Create an *admin* user. In the following example, the admin user is *superMan* and has the role `userAdminAnyDatabase`, which grants the rights to add, edit, or remove database users for any database:

```
                                    zed@zed: ~
File Edit View Search Terminal Help
> use admin;
switched to db admin
> db.createUser(
...    {
...       user: "superMan",
...       pwd: "up.up.and.away!",
...       roles: [ { role: "userAdminAnyDatabase", db: "admin" } ]
...    }
... );
Successfully added user: {
        "user" : "superMan",
        "roles" : [
                {
                        "role" : "userAdminAnyDatabase",
                        "db" : "admin"
                }
        ]
}
>
```

- Restart mongod with security.
  You can either use the mongod command switch --auth, or add the following to
  the MongoDB config file:

  ```
  security:
      authorization: enabled
  ```

Once you have performed this simple procedure, you can then connect to MongoDB
according to your infrastructure requirements. If you then wish to perform *any* actions,
however, you will need to authenticate.

To find out who, from the *mongo* shell, can run this, use the following
command: db.runCommand({connectionStatus:1});.

Database privilege actions

Before creating database roles and assigning users, it's a good idea to become familiar with
the various database *privilege actions* which can be assigned. Privilege actions represent
operations that a role can perform on a *resource*. A resource can be a collection, database,
or cluster. Each privilege allows the role to run the database command(s) associated with
that privilege.

The resource `anyResource` is reserved and gives access to all resources in your system. Designed mainly for internal use, its use is not recommended as it could potentially introduce a major security vulnerability.

Privilege actions pertain specifically to *database* commands, and are not to be confused with *mongo* shell methods. The latter, for the most part, are wrappers for database commands. For example, the *mongo* shell method `db.collection.aggregate()` is actually a wrapper for the database `aggregate()` command. Likewise, the database `find()` command is leveraged by the *mongo* shell methods `db.collection.find()`, `findOne()`, `findAndModify()`, and so on.

CRUD privilege actions

Here is a summary of the more important privileges associated with create, read, update, and delete operations:

- `find`: Allows the role to run database commands such as `aggregate()`, `find()`, `group()`, `count()`, and `mapReduce()`.
- `insert`: Allows the role to perform the `insert()` and `create()` database commands (and their equivalents). It should be noted that when using the `$out` aggregation pipeline stage operator, or `mapReduce()`, this privilege is needed as well.
- `remove`: Allows the role to perform the `delete()` command. In addition, certain commands require this in secondary stages (for example, `db.collection.findAndModify()`), as well as when using the `$out` aggregation pipeline stage operator, or `mapReduce()`.

- `update`: Allows the role to perform the `update()` database command. In addition, just as with remove, commands requiring an update in their secondary stages need this privilege as well.

Database management privilege actions

Commands in this category deal with database user administration, including the ability to grant permissions. Examples of some of the more important privilege actions are listed here:

- `changePassword`: Grants the ability to change user passwords
- `createCollection`, `createIndex`, `createRole`, and `createUser`: Ability to create collections, indexes, roles, and users
- `dropDatabase`, `dropCollection`, `dropRole`, and `dropUser`: Ability to remove collections, indexes, roles, and users

Infrastructure privilege actions

The remaining sets of privileges can be collectively identified as dealing with the infrastructure of your MongoDB system, such as administration of replication, sharding, and so on. Here is a summary of some of the more important privileges:

- `replSetConfigure`, `replSetGetConfig`, `replSetGetStatus`, `replSetHeartBeat`, and `replSetStateChange`: Allows the role to manage a replica set.
- `enableSharding`, `addShard`, `removeShard`, and `listShards`: Allows the role control over a sharded cluster.
- `moveChunk` and `splitChunks`: Gives the role control over chunks, the basic unit which governs how documents are distributed between shards.
- `closeAllDatabases`, `repairDatabase`, `reIndex`, and `shutdown`: Gives the role control over the database server instance.
- `setFreeMonitoring`: Gives the role the ability to enable or disable *free monitoring* (`https://docs.mongodb.com/manual/administration/free-monitoring/#free-monitoring`) of either standalone or replica sets in the cloud.
- `serverStatus`: Allows the role to view information on the database server.
- `anyAction` and `internalAction`: Allows the role any action on that resource. Use with caution!

Role-based access control

It's important to note the difference between a *role* (`https://docs.mongodb.com/manual/core/authorization/#role-based-access-control`) and a *user*. Privileges are granted to *roles*. Roles, in turn, are assigned to *users*. This arrangement vastly minimizes the complications which could arise as the numbers of database users increases. In addition, one role can inherit from another, which allows you to create a hierarchy of privileges and minimize the number of assignments which need to be made.

Built-in roles

MongoDB includes a number of built-in roles (`https://docs.mongodb.com/manual/core/security-built-in-roles/#built-in-roles`) for administration convenience, and the most important are summarized here:

Role	Allows User To ...
read	Read the database (for example, execute `db.collection.find()`)
readWrite	Create, read, update, and delete data
userAdmin	Perform user administration for a given database
userAdminAnyDatabase	Perform user administration for all databases
clusterAdmin	Manage and monitor clusters and hosts within the cluster
backup	restore	Perform database backups and restores
readWriteAnyDatabase	Create, read, update, and delete any database
root	Shortcut to assigning all ***AnyDatabase** privileges

Custom roles

You can use the `db.createRole(<role document>)` method to create custom roles. The *role document* fields include the following:

Role	Name of the new role
privileges	Identifies the *resource* and *actions*. *Resource* identifies the database and/or collection.
roles	Any built-in or already-existing roles.
authenticationRestrictions	Whitelist allowed IP addresses or **CIDR (Classless Inter-Domain Routing,** `https://en.wikipedia.org/wiki/Classless_Inter-Domain_Routing`) ranges (optional).

In the following example, we are creating a role `purchases` which only allows create, read, update, and delete operations on the `purchases` collection. Otherwise, this role is allowed to read from the `sweetscomplete` database. This role also restricts access to IP address `192.168.2.107`:

```
> use admin;
switched to db admin
> db.createRole(
... {
...    role: "purchasing",
...    privileges: [
...        { resource: { db: "sweetscomplete", collection: "purchases" },
...          actions: [ "find", "update", "insert", "remove" ] }
...    ],
...    roles: [ { role: "read", db: "sweetscomplete" } ],
...    authenticationRestrictions: [
...        {
...          clientSource: ["192.168.2.107"],
...          serverAddress: ["192.168.2.107"]
...        }
...    ]
... });
```

Database user administration

You can create database users to suit the purposes of administration and also to control access from applications that are using MongoDB programming language drivers. Here is a list of the more important *mongo shell database commands* that are used to manage users:

- `db.getUser("<name>")`: Retrieves information on user `<name>`
- `db.createUser(<user document>)`: Creates a user
- `db.changeUserPassword("<name>", "<new password>")`: Changes password for existing user `<name>`
- `db.updateUser("<name>",<update document>)`: Updates user `<name>` with the information in `<update document>`
- `db.dropUser("<name>")`: Removes user `<name>` from the database

In the following example, we are creating a user called `sweetsBasic` who has `readWrite` privileges in the `sweetscomplete` database:

```
                            zed@zed: ~
File  Edit  View  Search  Terminal  Help
> use sweetscomplete;
switched to db sweetscomplete
> db.createUser(
...    {
...       user: "sweetBasic",
...       pwd: "some.password",
...       roles: [ { role: "readWrite", db: "sweetscomplete" } ]
...    }
... );
Successfully added user: {
        "user" : "sweetBasic",
        "roles" : [
                {
                        "role" : "readWrite",
                        "db" : "sweetscomplete"
                }
        ]
}
>
```

When you execute `db.createUser()`, the user is added to the currently used database. This becomes the *authentication database* for that user. Otherwise, you can create users by using the default authentication database *admin*. Doing so does not prevent assigning that user privileges in other databases.

Summary

In this chapter, you learned about the different aspects of security in a MongoDB installation. After an initial overview, you learned about transport layer security, and how to configure MongoDB for TLS/SSL. After that, you learned about the different authentication mechanisms available, including SCRAM and x.509 certificates. You also learned about Kerberos and LDAP, which are only available in the MongoDB Enterprise Edition. After that, you learned how to enable authentication and create an admin user. You then learned about the various database privilege actions which can be applied to roles. You also learned about some of the built-in roles and how to define your own. Finally, you learned how to create database users and assign them to one or more roles.

In the next chapter, you will be given a walkthrough of a complete application based upon MongoDB, including capturing web form data to be inserted into the database, retrieving query information from MongoDB and putting it into a jQuery *DataTable*, and providing support for transactions.

8

Getting from a Web Form to MongoDB

In this chapter, we return once again to programming language drivers. You will learn what is involved in making a query using jQuery data tables for a PHP program which accesses a MongoDB database on the backend. You will then see how a new purchase is added using jQuery autocomplete fields, that is, by making AJAX queries via PHP to the MongoDB database, thus returning a JSON response. As part of the insert process, you will learn how to invoke transaction `support`*, embed customer and product documents into a purchase document, and add an entry to an embedded array. In addition, we will discuss adding x.509 certificates and authentication and access control.

The demo server used for this chapter is running Ubuntu Linux 18.04.

The topics to be covered in this chapter are as follows:

- Building the application
- Configuring transaction support
- Adding security

* Transaction support is only available in MongoDB v4.0 and above.

Building the application

The first step in building the application is to make sure that the underlying programming driver infrastructure is in place. This has already been covered in detail in Chapter 4, *Developing with Program Language Drivers*. Here is a brief overview of the steps to take:

1. Install *PHP X.Y* and the phpX.Y-dev library, where X.Y is the target version (for example, PHP 7.2)
2. Install *PECL* by installing php-pear
3. Install the PHP mongodb extension using pecl
4. Install the PHP MongoDB Library using the composer require mongodb/mongodb command

Once the programming language driver infrastructure is in place, we can turn our attention to application development. The objective in this illustration is to provide a way to view and add purchases using the sweetscomplete database. To refresh your memory, the purchases document appears as follows:

```
fred@fred-linux: ~/Desktop/Repos/MongoDB-Quick-Start-Guide-Doug
test@fred-linux[up:2174]> use sweetscomplete;
switched to db sweetscomplete
sweetscomplete@fred-linux[up:2174]> db.purchases.findOne();
{
        "_id" : ObjectId("5b500ad7533b844173064582"),
        "customer" : {
                "_id" : ObjectId("5b482b45533b843e7b6f70c3"),
                "name" : "Conrad Perry",
                "state_province" : "QC",
                "country" : "CA",
                "balance" : 745.32
        },
        "product" : {
                "_id" : ObjectId("5b4c232accf2ea73a85ed2c7"),
                "sku" : "C22000",
                "title" : "Chocolate Toaster Tarts",
                "price" : 2.2
        },
        "date" : "2017-09-20",
        "quantity" : 15,
        "amount" : 33
}
sweetscomplete@fred-linux[up:2174]>
```

We will first turn our attention to the initial view.

Defining the initial view

The initial view will be presented by index.php, which is located in the web server's document root. We include the Composer autoloader, initialize the variables, and set up the URL used by the view template index.phtml to make a jQuery DataTables query:

```
// autoloading
 include __DIR__ . '/../vendor/autoload.php';
 use Application\Base;
 $start_date = 'now';
 $end_date = '';
 $limit = Base::DEFAULT_LIMIT;
 $ajax = Base::buildUrl($start_date, $end_date, $limit);
 include __DIR__ . '/index.phtml';
```

The Application\Base class is extended by three services classes which make the connection to the MongoDB database, perform lookups, and ultimately insert data. Autoloading is provided by Composer, which means that we need to identify the Application namespace in the composer.json file:

```
{ "require": { "mongodb/mongodb": "*" },
     "autoload": { "psr-4": {"Application\\": "Application"} } }
```

The actual presentation of the initial page is performed by the view script index.phtml. Here, we break down the more important items in this file. In the <head> part of the document, we load the jQuery DataTables stylesheet:

```
<link rel="stylesheet"
href="https://cdn.datatables.net/1.10.19/css/jquery.dataTables.min.css">
```

Just before the closing </body> tag, we load the minimal jQuery JavaScript needed, and define a $(document).ready() function that invokes jQuery DataTables:

```
<script src="https://code.jquery.com/jquery-3.3.1.js"></script>
<script
src="https://cdn.datatables.net/1.10.19/js/jquery.dataTables.min.js"></scri
pt>
<script>
 $(document).ready(function() {
 $('#purchases').DataTable( {
 "ajax": "<?= $ajax ?>"
 } ); } );
</script>
```

Note that the source of the data is $ajax, which was defined in the index.php file as the static call Base::buildUrl($start_date, $end_date, $limit), which we cover in the subsection on the Main class.

The DataTables component in the initial page is a simple HTML table minus the supporting rows:

```
<table id="purchases" class="display" style="width:100%">
  <thead>
     <tr><th>Customer</th><th>Prod
Title</th><th>Amount</th><th>Date</th></tr>
  </thead>
</table>
```

Finally, we provide a form where the fictitious administrator can narrow down the search by specifying start and end dates, as well as a limit on how many search results are returned:

```
<form name="dates" method="get" action="/index.php" id="date_search">
 <table><tr>
     <td>Start</td><td><input type="date" name="start_date" value="<?=
$start_date ?>" /></td>
     <td>End</td><td><input type="date" name="end_date" value="<?=
$end_date ?>" /></td>
     <td>Limit</td><td>
         <input type="number" name="limit" value="<?= $limit ?>"
style="width:50px;"/></td>
     <td><input type="submit" name="submit" value="Search" class="button
marT5" /></td>
     <td><a href="/add.php">NEW PURCHASE</a></td>
 </tr></table>
 </form>
```

Here is a screenshot of the initial page:

Defining the Add Purchase view

The form target action is `add.php`, which defines the view in which we add a purchase. It is much more complicated, of course, as we need to capture form post data and perform a database insertion. The actual insert is performed by the `Add` service class.

First, we activate autoloading, and retrieve parameters from `init.php`:

```
include __DIR__ . '/../vendor/autoload.php';
use Application\Add;
$name    = '';
$sku     = '';
$qty     = 1;
$product = '';
$params  = include __DIR__ . '/../Application/init.php';
```

The parameters supplied by `init.php` will allows us to add authentication support, which we will discuss later. We then intercept and sanitize the `name`, `sku`, and `quantity` parameters from the form posting. The `Add` class is used to lookup the customer and product information, and also to save the purchase. If successful, we redirect to home:

```
if ($name && $sku) {
    $quantity = (isset($_POST['quantity'])) ? (int) $_POST['quantity'] :
1;
    $service = new Add(params);
    $customerDoc = $service->findCustomerByName($name);
    $productDoc = $service->findProductBySku($sku);
    if ($service->savePurchase($customerDoc, $productDoc, $quantity)) {
        header('Location: /');
        exit;
    } else {
        $message = 'Unable to process purchase';
    }
}
include __DIR__ . '/add.phtml';
```

To conserve space, we only cover pertinent aspects of the `add.phtml` view script. We use the jQuery UI autocomplete widget to provide lookups for customers and products. These are placed in the `<head>` portion of the HTML page:

```
<link rel="stylesheet"
href="//code.jquery.com/ui/1.12.1/themes/base/jquery-ui.css">
 <script src="https://code.jquery.com/jquery-1.12.4.js"></script>
 <script src="https://code.jquery.com/ui/1.12.1/jquery-ui.js"></script>
 <script>
 $( function() {
     $( "#names" ).autocomplete({
       source: "/json.php?cust_name=1", minLength: 1 });
     $( "#products" ).autocomplete({
       source: "/json.php?prod_title=1", minLength: 1 });
   });
 </script>
```

The form is a simple HTML form, with the customer and product inputs being provided by jQuery autocomplete:

```
<form action="add.php" method="post" >
     <table style="width:50%;">
     <tr><th>Customer</th>
         <td><input id="names" name="name" value="<?= $name ?>" /></td>
     </tr><tr>
         <th>Product</th>
         <td><input id="products" name="product" value="<?= $product ?>"
/></td>
     </tr><tr>
         <th>Quantity</th>
         <td><input type="number" id="quantity" name="quantity" value="<?=
$qty ?>" /></td>
     </tr></table>
     <input type="submit" name="add" value="Add Purchase" class="button
marT5" />
     <input type="submit" name="cancel" value="Cancel" class="button marT5"
/>
  </form>
```

Here is a screenshot of the **Add Purchase** page. The outer frame is the same. The inner frame shows the product's autocomplete:

Defining the JSON response script

Both the initial view and the add purchase view use jQuery to make an AJAX request to a script called `json.php`. This script uses the `Lookup` service class to perform lookups and return results in JSON format. The `Base` and `Main` are used for URL parameter capture and URL formulation. As with the other two core scripts, we initiate autoloading. As with the add script, we retrieve parameters from `Application\init.php` (described in the next section):

```
include __DIR__ . '/../vendor/autoload.php';
use Application\ {Base,Lookup,Main};
$params   = include __DIR__ . '/../Application/init.php';
$service = new Lookup($params);
```

The `$term` is provided by jQuery when our fictitious admin starts typing `$term = (isset($_GET['term'])) ? strip_tags($_GET['term']) : '';`. We then check to see if we need to lookup the customer name, product title, or purchases by date:

```
$output = [];
 try {
     if (isset($_GET['cust_name'])) {
         $output = $service->getListOfCustomers($term);
     } elseif (isset($_GET['prod_title'])) {
         $output = $service->getListOfProducts($term);
     } else {
         // get start/end dates + limit from URL (if any)
         $start_date = 'now';
         $end_date   = '';
         $limit      = Base::DEFAULT_LIMIT;
         Main::getUrlParams($start_date, $end_date, $limit);
         $output = ['data' =>
$service->getListOfPurchasesByDate($start_date, $end_date, $limit)];
     }
```

We wrap everything in a `try { } catch() { }` block in case of any errors:

```
 } catch (Throwable $e) {
     error_log(__METHOD__ . ':' . $e->getMessage());
     $output = 'ERROR: look at the error log for more information';
 }
```

And finally, the output is converted to JSON using the PHP function `json_encode()`:

```
echo json_encode($output);
```

This completes our coverage of the core scripts. Now, it's time to look at the `Connection` class, which is used by the service classes.

Defining the Connection class

The main task of the `Connection` class is to produce an instance of `MongoDB\Client`. We do not show the class constants which represent error messages in order to conserve space. We start by defining the namespace and external classes to use:

```
namespace Application;
 use Exception;
 use MongoDB\Client as MongoClient;
 class Connection {
```

The `__construct()` method accepts a configuration array as an argument, and produces the `MongoDB\Client` and `MongoDB\Driver\Manager` instances:

```
    protected $mongoClient;
     protected $manager;      // MongoDB\Driver\Manager
     public function __construct($config) {
         if (!isset($config['uri'])) {
             throw new Exception(self::ERROR_CONFIG_URI);
         }
         $uriOpts = $config['uriOpts'] ?? [];
         $driverOpts = $config['driverOpts'] ?? [];
         $uri = $this->buildUri($config);
         $this->mongoClient = new MongoClient($uri, $uriOpts, $driverOpts);
         $this->manager = $this->mongoClient->getManager();
     }
```

We then provide `get*()` methods to retrieve the client, manager, and session (used for transaction support, which is discussed later):

```
    public function getClient() { return $this->mongoClient; }
     public function getManager() { return $this->manager; }
     public function getSession() { return $this->manager->startSession(); }
 }
```

The `buildUri()` method is used to accept configuration and produce a MongoDB connection string (https://docs.mongodb.com/manual/reference/connection-string/ #standard-connection-string-format). As an example, the target string might appear as follows:

```
mongodb://[username:password@]host1[:port1][/[database][?options]]
```

Here is the `buildUri()` method in full:

```
public function buildUri($config) {
    $uri = 'mongodb://';
    if (isset($config['uri']['username']) &&
isset($config['uri']['password']))
        $uri .= $config['uri']['username'] . ':' .
$config['uri']['password'] . '@';
    if (!isset($config['uri']['host'])) throw new
Exception(self::ERROR_HOST);
    $uri .= $config['uri']['host'];
    $uri .= (isset($config['uri']['port'])) ? ':' . $config['uri']['port']
: '';
    $uri .= (isset($config['uri']['database'])) ? '/' .
$config['uri']['database'] : '';
    if (isset($config['uriOpts'])) {
        if (!is_array($config['uriOpts'])) throw new
Exception(self::ERROR_OPTS);
        $uri .= '?';
        foreach ($config['uriOpts'] as $key => $value)
            $uri .= $key . '=' . $value . '&';
        $uri = substr($uri, 0, -1);    // trim trailing '&'
    }
    return $uri;
}
```

Defining the service classes

Next, we define the service classes `Main`, `Lookup`, and `Add`. These classes contain the following supporting logic:

- `Main`: Capturing URL parameters and building an AJAX target URL for the initial view
- `Lookup`: Performing purchases lookups
- `Add`: Saving a new purchase

First, we will examine the `Base` class, which all three service classes extend.

Application\Base

The `Application\Base` class contains logic needed by the three service classes `Main`, `Lookup`, and `Add`. As with `Connection`, we define this class in the `Application` namespace. In this class, we provide useful constants and properties which represent the database collections `products`, `purchases`, and `customers`. We also provide access to the `Application\Connection` instance:

```
namespace Application;
 class Base {
     const DATE_FORMAT = 'Y-m-d';
     const DEFAULT_URL = '/json.php';
     const DEFAULT_LIMIT = 100;
     const DEFAULT_END_DATE = 'P99Y';
     protected $connection;
     protected $products;
     protected $purchases;
     protected $customers;
     public function __construct($config) {
         $this->connection = new Connection($config);
         $client = $this->connection->getClient();
         $this->products = $client->sweetscomplete->products;
         $this->purchases = $client->sweetscomplete->purchases;
         $this->customers = $client->sweetscomplete->customers;
     }
     public function getConnection() { return $this->connection; }
 }
```

We now turn our attention to the three main service classes, starting with `Main`.

Application\Main

This class consists of two static calls to methods which capture and sanitize URL parameters, and a helper method. It is used by both `index.php` as well as `json.php`:

```
namespace Application;
 use DateTime;
 use DateInterval;
 class Main extends Base {
```

The first method calls the second one, and builds the URL which is then used by jQuery DataTables as its AJAX target:

```
public static function buildUrl(&$start_date, &$end_date, &$limit) {
        self::getUrlParams($start_date, $end_date, $limit);
        return self::DEFAULT_URL . '?start_date=' . $start_date
```

```
                                   . '&end_date=' . $end_date . '&limit=' . $limit;
        }
```

The second method captures and sanitizes URL parameters which represent start and end dates, plus the results limit:

```
    public static function getUrlParams(&$start_date, &$end_date, &$limit) :
void {
        $start_date = (isset($_GET['start_date']))
                    ? strip_tags($_GET['start_date']) :
date(self::DATE_FORMAT);
        $end_date   = (isset($_GET['end_date'])) ?
strip_tags($_GET['end_date'])    : '';
        $limit      = (isset($_GET['limit'])) ? (int) $_GET['limit'] :
self::DEFAULT_LIMIT;
        $end_date   = self::calcEndDate($start_date, $end_date);
        }
```

The third and last method is used to calculate the end date if one is not specified:

```
    public static function calcEndDate($start_date, $end_date = '') {
        // end date
        if (!$end_date) {
            $startDateObj = new DateTime($start_date);
            $endDateObj = new DateTime('now');
            $endDateObj->add(new DateInterval(self::DEFAULT_END_DATE));
            $end_date = $endDateObj->format(self::DATE_FORMAT);
        }
        return $end_date;
        }
    }
```

Next, we examine the Lookup class.

Application\Lookup

The Lookup class is used by json.php to perform purchases lookups by date in the initial view. When adding a new purchase, the same class provides responses to requests that were originated by the jQuery autocomplete widget for customer names and product titles:

```
namespace Application;
 use Throwable;
 use MongoDB\BSON\Regex;
 class Lookup extends Base {
```

The first method returns an array of customer names. The $term is provided by the jQuery autocompete widget when the user starts typing:

```php
public function getListOfCustomers($term) {
    $filter = NULL;
    if ($term) {
        $regex = new Regex($term, 'i');
        $filter = ['name' => $regex];
    }
    $options = [ 'sort' => ['name' => 1], 'projection' => ['name' =>
1] ];
    $result  = [];
    try {
        $cursor = $this->find($this->customers, $filter, $options);
        foreach ($cursor as $document)
            $result[$document->name] = $document->name;
    } catch (Throwable $e) {
        error_log(__METHOD__ . ':' . $e->getMessage());
        $result[] = 'ERROR: unable to find customers';
    }
    return $result;
}
```

The next method is similar except that it produces an array of product titles:

```php
public function getListOfProducts($term) {
    $filter = NULL;
    if ($term) {
        $regex = new Regex($term, 'i');
        $filter = ['title' => $regex];
    }
    $options = ['sort' => ['title' => 1], 'projection' => ['sku' => 1,
'title' => 1] ];
    $result  = [];
    try {
        $cursor = $this->find($this->products, $filter, $options);
        foreach ($cursor as $document)
            $result[] = $document->title . ' [' . $document->sku .
']';
    } catch (Throwable $e) {
        error_log(__METHOD__ . ':' . $e->getMessage());
        $result[] = 'ERROR: unable to find products';
    }
    return $result;
}
```

The third method builds a filter with start and end dates. It also adds a limit to the number of purchase documents produced:

```php
    public function getListOfPurchasesByDate($start_date, $end_date, $limit
= self::DEFAULT_LIMIT) {
        if ($end_date) {
            $filter  = [
                '$and' => [
                    ['date' => ['$gte' => $start_date]],
                    ['date' => ['$lte' => $end_date]]
                ]
            ];
        } else {
            $filter  = [ 'date' => ['$gte' => $start_date] ];
        }
        $options = [
            'limit' => $limit,
            'sort'  => ['date' => 1],
            'projection' => ['customer.name' => 1, 'product.title' => 1,
'amount' => 1, 'date' => 1]
        ];
        $result  = [];
        try {
            $cursor = $this->find($this->purchases, $filter, $options);
            foreach ($cursor as $document)
                $result[] = [$document->customer->name,
                             $document->product->title,
                             sprintf('%.2f', $document->amount),
                             $document->date];
        } catch (Throwable $e) {
            error_log(__METHOD__ . ':' . $e->getMessage());
            $result[] = 'ERROR: unable to find purchases for these dates';
        }
        return $result;
    }
```

The last method provides a wrapper for the MongoDB `find()` method:

```php
    public function find($collection, $filter = NULL, array $options = []) {
        $result = [];
        if ($filter && $options) {
            $result = $collection->find($filter, $options);
        } elseif ($options && !$filter) {
            $result = $collection->find([], $options);
        } elseif ($filter && !$options) {
            $result = $collection->find($filter);
        } else {
            $result = $collection->find();
```

```
        }
        return $result;
    }
}
```

Finally, we finish this set by examining Add.

Application\Add

This class performs operations that are needed to store a purchase: lookup the customer and product, create and save the purchase document, and then update the purchase history array in the customer document:

```
namespace Application;
  use Throwable;
  use MongoDB\Model\BSONDocument;
  class Add extends Base {
```

The first method performs a customer lookup by *name*. Note that we define a *projection* which represents a limited subset of all customer information. This becomes the base customer document which will later be embedded in the purchase document:

```
public function findCustomerByName($name) {
    $options = [ 'projection' => [
        '_id' => 1, 'name' => 1, 'state_province' => 1,
        'country' => 1, 'balance' => 1, 'purch_history' => 1 ] ];
    $result   = NULL;
    try {
        $result = $this->customers->findOne(['name' => $name],
$options);
    } catch (Throwable $e) {
        error_log(__METHOD__ . ':' . $e->getMessage());
    }
    return $result;
}
```

Next, we do the same thing for product, performing a lookup based on the sku number. We pull all product information except *description*:

```
public function findProductBySku($sku) {
    $options = ['projection' => ['description' => 0]];
    $result   = NULL;
    try {
        $result = $this->products->findOne(['sku' => $sku], $options);
    } catch (Throwable $e) {
        error_log(__METHOD__ . ':' . $e->getMessage());
```

```
        }
        return $result;
    }
```

Next, we define a method which creates the purchase document and saves it:

```
public function savePurchase(BSONDocument $customer, BSONDocument $product,
$quantity) {
        $result = FALSE;
        $date = date(self::DATE_FORMAT);
        $session = $this->connection->getSession();
        $data = [ 'customer' => $customer, 'product' => $product, 'date'
=> $date,
                    'quantity' => $quantity, 'amount' => $quantity * (float)
$product->price ];
        try {
            if ($result = $this->purchases->insertOne($data)) {
```

We also add logic to add the purchase date to the embedded purchase history array, and update the customer document:

```
            $list = $customer->purch_history;
            $list[] = $date;
            $this->customers->updateOne(
                ['name' => $customer->name],
                ['$set' => ['purch_history' => $list]]);
            }
        } catch (Throwable $e) {
            $result = FALSE;
            error_log(__METHOD__ . ':' . $e->getMessage());
        }
        return $result;
    }
```

In order to provide support for *transactions* (https://docs.mongodb.com/manual/core/transactions/#transactions), which is only available in MongoDB 4.0 and above, we need to get a MongoDB\Driver\Session instance from the connection. We then supply it as an argument to the insert and update operations. Here is the same method that we used previously but with transaction support added:

```
public function savePurchaseWithSession($customer, $product, $quantity)
{
        $result = FALSE;
        $date = date(self::DATE_FORMAT);
        // get MongoDB\Driver\Session instance needed for transaction
support
        $session = $this->connection->getSession();
        $data = [ 'customer' => $customer, 'product' => $product, 'date'
```

```
=> $date,
                        'quantity' => $quantity, 'amount'    => $quantity *
(float) $product->price ];
          try {
              // begin transaction
              $session->startTransaction();
              // need to add session as an option to get transaction support
              if ($result = $this->purchases->insertOne($data, ['session' =>
$session])) {
                    $list = $customer->purch_history;
                    $list[] = $date;
                    $this->customers->updateOne(
                        ['name' => $customer->name],
                        ['$set' => ['purch_history' => $list]],
                        // need to add session as an option to get transaction
support
                        ['session' => $session]);
              }
              // commit
              $session->commitTransaction();
          } catch (Throwable $e) {
              // rollback
              $session->abortTransaction();
              $result = FALSE;
              error_log(__METHOD__ . ':' . $e->getMessage());
          }
          return $result;
      }
  }
```

Configuring transaction support

In addition to getting a `MongoDB\Driver\Session` instance and supplying it as an argument to the `insert()` and `update()` methods, we must also provide the appropriate configuration. In the demonstration application, `json.php` and `add.php` both pulled connection parameters from a file called `Application/init.php`. The basic configuration for a simple MongoDB database with no security is as follows:

```
return [
    'uri' => [
        'host' => '127.0.0.1',
        'database' => 'sweetscomplete'
    ]
];
```

In order to provide support for transactions, we must run the operation on a MongoDB replica set member. The revised configuration file, Application\init.php, would appear as follows:

```
return [
    'uri' => [
        'host' => '192.168.2.107',
        'database' => 'sweetscomplete',
        'port' => 27017,
    ],
    'uriOpts' => [
        'replicaSet' => 'sweets_11',
    ],
];
```

Our Application\Connection::buildUri() method will then create the following MongoDB connection string:

```
mongodb://192.168.2.107:27017/sweetscomplete?replicaSet=sweets_11
```

We must also add to the MongoDB config file and ensure that the MongoDB instance is a member of the replica set:

```
replication:
    replSetName: "sweets_11"

net:
    port: 27017
    bindIp: 0.0.0.0
```

Finally, add.php needs to be modified to call Application\Add::savePurchaseWithSession(), which provides transaction support:

```
if ($service->savePurchaseWithSession($customerDoc, $productDoc,
$quantity)) {
    header('Location: /');
    exit;
} else {
    $message = '<h1 style="color:red;">Unable to process purchase</h1>';
}
```

Adding security

As with transactions, when adding security, we need to modify the MongoDB connection string. Assuming that we are using x.509 certificates, and assuming that we have created a database user `zed`, here is the modified `Application/init.php` file:

```
return [
    'uri' => [
        'host' => 'mongod',
        'database' => 'sweetscomplete',
        'username' => 'zed',
        'password' => 'password',
    ],
    'uriOpts' => [
        'ssl' => true,
        'replicaSet' => 'sweets_11',
        'authSource' => 'admin',
    ],
    'driverOpts' => [
        'ca_file' => '/etc/ssl/ca.pem',
        'pem_file' => '/etc/ssl/zed.pem',
        'pem_pwd' => 'password',
    ],
];
```

And this is the connect string which is produced:

```
mongodb://zed:password@mongod/sweetscomplete?ssl=1&replicaSet=sweets_11&aut
hSource=admin
```

The MongoDB conf file also needs to be modified, as described in Chapter 7, *Securing MongoDB*:

```
net:
  port: 27017
  bindIp: 0.0.0.0

net:
  ssl:
      mode: requireSSL
      PEMKeyFile: /etc/ssl/mongod.pem
      PEMKeyPassword: "password"
      CAFile: /etc/ssl/ca.pem

security:
  authorization: enabled

setParameter:
  authenticationMechanisms: PLAIN,SCRAM-SHA-256,MONGODB-X509
```

Summary

In this chapter, you learned how to configure a PHP-based application which performs jQuery lookups, queries the MongoDB database, and produces a JSON response. You also learned how to configure the application to provide support for transactions and security. Among the techniques demonstrated here, you learned how to embed documents and update an embedded array.

This chapter concludes this book. The purpose of this book is to present you with enough information to get a MongoDB installation up and running in a safe and secure manner. Along the way, we also showed you some of the advanced features that are unique to MongoDB such as the aggregation pipeline, replication, and sharding. It is our hope that you will find this book a useful addition to your reference library, and that it encourages you to explore other Packt books in this series.

Using Docker

Using MongoDB with Docker

The installation of *Docker* (`https://www.docker.com/`) and how it operates is beyond the scope of this book. It will be of interest to DevOps (in other words, developers and IT operations professionals) to know that the Docker community has created an image (`https://hub.docker.com/_/mongo/`) in which MongoDB is pre-installed. To use this image, assuming that you have Docker installed, proceed as follows:

1. Go to the GitHub page for the Docker mongo image (`https://github.com/docker-library/docs/blob/master/mongo/README.md`), and choose a tag to use. The list of tags refer to different versions of Windows and Ubuntu Linux. Each tag listed on the GitHub page links to a `docker` file, so if you are not running either Windows or Ubuntu Linux, it's easy enough to modify the `docker` file to suit your needs.

2. From the Command Prompt/Terminal window, issue this command, where **<tag>** is the one chosen in the preceding step and `<container-name>` is the name you choose for your local container:

```
docker run --name <container> -d mongo:<tag>
```

3. In the example we show here, the container name is `mongo-test` and the tag is `4.1.2-xenial`, which corresponds to Ubuntu Linux version 16.x and MongoDB version 4.1.2:

```
fred@fred-linux:~$ sudo docker run --name mongo-test -d mongo:4.1.2-xenial
[sudo] password for fred:
Unable to find image 'mongo:4.1.2-xenial' locally
4.1.2-xenial: Pulling from library/mongo
3b37166ec614: Already exists
ba077e1ddb3a: Already exists
34c83d2bc656: Already exists
84b69b6e4743: Already exists
0f72e97e1f61: Already exists
ce9080750e9c: Already exists
931490877d83: Already exists
ab49899969a7: Already exists
a0ef762c0966: Already exists
bcb5a38b487c: Pull complete
05dec482edf5: Pull complete
51f39fd6ccb8: Pull complete
d7e3546d7fb8: Pull complete
94bc5c4b9673: Pull complete
Digest: sha256:206a752b1b87013932a69ef2b619f7cbf144d7465b0beeae3edbadb0241f2fe2
Status: Downloaded newer image for mongo:4.1.2-xenial
29d1719dc70c9145bffa687a16ad3c1a984629b2ffb49c71c9ff885920dc1a7d
fred@fred-linux:~$
```

4. You can then run a *mongo* shell off the container using the `exec` command to launch a `bash` shell, as shown here:

```
fred@fred-linux:~$ sudo docker exec -it mongo-test bash
root@29d1719dc70c:/# mongo
MongoDB shell version v4.1.2
connecting to: mongodb://127.0.0.1:27017
MongoDB server version: 4.1.2
Welcome to the MongoDB shell.
```

5. At this point, you can run any *mongo* shell command, including those needed to create databases, collections, queries, and so on.

Other Books You May Enjoy

If you enjoyed this book, you may be interested in these other books by Packt:

MongoDB Administrator's Guide
Cyrus Dasadia

ISBN: 978-1-78398-674-3

- Install and deploy MongoDB in production
- Manage and implement optimal indexes
- Optimize monitoring in MongoDB
- Fine-tune the performance of your queries
- Debug and diagnose your database's performance
- Optimize database backups and recovery and ensure high availability
- Make your MongoDB instance scalable
- Implement security and user authentication features in MongoDB
- Master optimal cloud deployment strategies

Mastering MongoDB 3.x
Alex Giamas

ISBN: 978-1-78398-260-8

- Get hands-on with advanced querying techniques such as indexing, expressions, arrays, and more.
- Configure, monitor, and maintain highly scalable MongoDB environment like an expert.
- Master replication and data sharding to optimize read/write performance.
- Design secure and robust applications based on MongoDB.
- Administer MongoDB-based applications on-premise or in the cloud
- Scale MongoDB to achieve your design goals
- Integrate MongoDB with big data sources to process huge amounts of data

Leave a review - let other readers know what you think

Please share your thoughts on this book with others by leaving a review on the site that you bought it from. If you purchased the book from Amazon, please leave us an honest review on this book's Amazon page. This is vital so that other potential readers can see and use your unbiased opinion to make purchasing decisions, we can understand what our customers think about our products, and our authors can see your feedback on the title that they have worked with Packt to create. It will only take a few minutes of your time, but is valuable to other potential customers, our authors, and Packt. Thank you!

Index

M

U

Ubuntu Linux
  MongoDB, installing on 14, 15

W

W3Techs
  reference 14
wide column
  reference 28
Windows

MongoDB, installing on 9, 10, 11

X

x.509 authentication
  about 137
  internal authentication 138
  Mongo shell authentication 137
x.509 certificates 132, 133

Y

yum (Yellowdog Updater, Modified) 19

Printed in Great Britain
by Amazon